" There I was...
flat on my back "

by

Bob Stevens

AERO PUBLISHERS, INC.
329 West Aviation Road, Fallbrook, CA 92028

Library of Congress Cataloging in Publication Data

Stevens, Bob, 1923-
    "There I was ... flat on my back."
    Includes the author's There I was and More there I
was.
    1. World War, 1939-1945—Humor, caricatures, etc.
2. American wit and humor, pictorial. 3. World War,
1939-1945—Songs and Music, American. I. Title.
D745.2.S773   358.4'00973   75-25247
ISBN 0-8168-8953-8

FOREWORD

That wise and wonderfully witty man, James Thurber (who was also among the world's all-time great cartoonists), once said, "Humor is a serious thing. I like to think of it as one of our greatest and earliest national resources which must be preserved at all times."

By that standard, Bob Stevens is a national resource. Those of us who are long-timers on the magazine have known this all along. Those of you who'll be meeting Bob for the first time will likely join us in that opinion after you've looked at only a few pages.

I don't know about you, but if you're an editor of a magazine and if, for more than ten years, you get not only quality art and genuinely funny material, invariably well done, but you also get it on time—why, you've got to think of anybody who can do all that as a national resource!

That first "There I Was"—back in January 1964—looks a little strange today. Bob's style has changed some in ten years. His drawing is a little cleaner these days, a little more polished, perhaps. But the one element that hasn't changed in this more than a decade is Bob's sense of humor, and for that let us all rejoice.

And let us all hope that there'll be still *another* ten years' worth of "There I Was", and lots more collections, like this one, of Bob's work in reprint. Let's see, there can be "Son of There I Was," and "There I Was Again," amd "I Was Still There," and perhaps eventually *"Was* I There?"

So, to Bob Stevens and to his many old friends and fans and to the new friends this book is bound to make for him, best wishes and happy landings from AIR FORCE Magazine—his original launch pad.

—Richard M. Skinner
Managing Editor, AIR FORCE MAGAZINE

INTRODUCTION

This book is laid out in reverse of the normal format — the *text* describes the *pictures*. There is just enough prose to set the stage or give a personal anecdote which might have inspired the drawing.

The drawings are not arranged in any chronological sequence — although an attempt has been made to group anecdotes by theatres of operation. You will find the Pacific area in the beginning of the book because that was the first overseas garden spot the author was sent at government expense; Europe came later (when I was damn near too old to enjoy it). There are some scattered sequences involving the missile and jet age. Since my military service extended into the post-WWII period, I felt that a dash of the "jet with it" era was in order.

This book also contains most of the songs, ballads, ditties and doggerel used by airmen during and subsequent to WW II. To my knowledge this is the first time a compendium of these marvelous bits of drollery have seen formal print. I know that I've left out favorites. It's impossible to get them all in a book of this size — or twice this size. Research through reams of yellowed, mimeographed "songbooks" of all three air services convinced me that at least these were the most duplicated (and, hence, most popular).

I was amazed by how prolific the fighter pilots were when it came to turning out material. They seemed to outnumber the bomber and transport types in volume by at least three to one. And another thing, the lads in Korea really surprised me. They were even more prolific than we older, WW II types. Maybe it was because Korea wasn't the "holy mission" kind of conflict that the second war was and they had more to gripe about. To prove that point, the Viet Nam thing produced the most vitriolic batch of bitchin', irreverent songs I've ever seen. Since this is, at best, a PG-rated book, I couldn't "sanitize" many of the Viet Nam songs for inclusion. Speaking of "sanitizing," I didn't think I had the right to alter any verse — those that appear are unabridged and straight.

As far as musical scores are concerned, the civilian counterpart is annotated — when known. The melodies are mostly of ancient vintage and your corner music store can usually supply the score. If you come across a song such as "I Wanted Wings" or "Come and Join the Air Force" where no tune is given and you can't remember the melody, take the book with you to the next gathering of the boys and ask around; chances are you'll find an old-timer who knows it. No tunes were indicated for much of the verse (or at least I couldn't find them) and, in many cases, music would be superfluous — the words say it all. For example, who needs music for "Let's Have a Party!"? (Editor's Note: You'll find an index of these deathless ditties in the back of the book.)

This, then, is the bawdy, lusty product of a griping lot. Humor and songs are, and always will be, an integral part of military life — just like early morning missions, hours and hours of waiting, long chow lines, drafty tents, dehydrated potatoes and dysentery. The men who inspired these cartoons and songs told it like it was. You can accept or ignore them, but you can't ignore the conditions that produced them.

— Bob Stevens

ACKNOWLEDGEMENTS

The author wishes to extend grateful thanks to all those who helped him in preparation of this book. Most especially, he wishes to thank Richard S. Skinner of the *Air Force* magazine for his cooperation and assistance.

Additionally, many readers of *Air Force* have contributed ideas for these cartoons. Space does not permit naming all these individuals—I can only offer as thanks this opportunity to share their humor with more readers through the medium of this book.

However, special thanks must be given to certain individuals and organizations who have aided "above and beyond." My deepest gratitude is extended to Capt. Bob Howard, USAF (Ret.), "The Ragged Irregulars" (91st Bomb Gp. (H)), The Confederate Air Force and Col. Edwin F. Carey, Jr., USAF (Ret.) for their contributions of humor and song.

The following bibliography may not be complete—as many of the songs are an amalgam of other printed works—but it covers a wide spectrum of time and the air services:

Songs of the Army Flyers, Pub. 1937 by Order of the Dadelians
Stovepipe Serenade, Vincent AFB, Arizona (1956)
The Air Corps Tactical School, Maxwell Field, Ala. (undated)
Songs of Squadron Officers' Course, Maxwell AFB (1953)
Fitron 174 'Hell Razors', (Navy) (undated)
Aces High, 317th FIS Songbook, Elmendorf AFB, Alaska (undated)
Songs to Drink By, 355 TFW Takhli RTAFB, Thailand

DEDICATION

This book is dedicated to the thousands of airmen in all services since World War I, who turned to humor and song to make their task easier.

I guess the place to begin is when you really face up to your personal role in airpower—for the first terrifying time—going overseas in wartime.

We rode 3,500 miles over the Pacific in a bucket-seat-equipped C-54 at 180 miles per hour. Later, we hit the beach of the smallest island I've ever seen in my life. We came in via Army landing craft just like the movies, wading ashore with our B4 bags balanced on our heads. Quite an inauspicious beginning for American Eagles who were going to "make the skies safe for democracy."

The "Cadet Daze" box you see on this and a few other pages recall those moments of unbounded glee as an aviation cadet.

B-32 DOMINATOR

HEAVY BOMBER
SPAN 135'   LENGTH 82' 11"

BESIDE A NEW GUINEA WATERFALL

Beside a New Guinea Waterfall
One bright and sunny day
Beside his shattered P-51
A young pursuiter lay.

His parachute hung from a nearby tree
He was not yet quite dead
So listen to the very last words
The young pursuiter said:

"Oh! I'm going to a better land
Where everything is right
Where whisky grows on telegraph poles
Play poker every night.

We haven't got a thing to do
But sit around and sing
Where all our crews are women
Oh! Death where is thy sting?"

Oh death where is thy sting - aling - aling?
Oh death where is thy sting - aling - aling?
The bells of Hell will ring - aling - aling
For you but not for *me*!

P-51 MUSTANG

FIGHTER
SPAN 37'   LENGTH 32' 3"

Back in the good old days—which is to say in the 1940s and through the 50s—sometimes there were more bad days than good. But now, in today's modern, streamlined, jet-propelled, worldwide air service, things are different. Aren't they?

The P-47 (affectionately called "the jug") shown on the adjoining page taking off from the atoll, could carry a bigger armament load than most light or medium bombers of the day. Consequently, they sometimes used 7,500 feet of a 6,000 foot runway.

Flak was invariably under-estimated by "intelligence" officers after poring over copious charts (these ground-pounder types almost all wore mustaches and skulked about with locked briefcases).

Inside tip: The little fighter pilots singing the bawdy "There are No Fighter Pilots Down in Hell" ballad will soon be set upon by the hulking 13th Air Force bomber pilot. (On some bases we had to have separate clubs for the bomber and fighter types. . . different temperaments, I guess.)

PV-I VENTURA

MEDIUM BOMBER
SPAN 65' 6"   LENGTH 51' 9"

NO ATOLL AT ALL

BANG

SPUT

POP

YEP! IT'S THE KITCHEN SINK

"LIGHT & INACCURATE" WAS WHAT HE SAID...

OH...THERE ARE NO FIGHTER PILOTS DOWN IN HELL...

CADET DAZE

OK MISTER! SHE'S ALL YOURS!

THE END OF A LONG, LONG DAY:

"SARGE, I THINK THAT CO_2 BOTTLE FROM MY DINGHY IS UP AROUND MY SHOULDER BLADES SOMEWHERE!"

COME AND JOIN THE AIR FORCE

Come on and join the Air Force and get your flying pay
You never have to work at all, just fly around all day
While others toil and study hard and soon grow old and blind
We'll take the air without a care and you will never mind.

CHORUS: You'll never mind, you'll never mind
          Oh, come and join the Air Force
          And you will never mind.

Come on and get promoted as high as you desire
You're riding on a gravy train when you're an Air Force flyer
But just when you're about to be a general you'll find
The engine coughs, the wings fall off, and you will never mind!

And when you loop and spin her and with an awful tear
You find yourself without your wings but you will never care
For in about two minutes more another pair you'll find
You'll fly with Pete and his angels sweet and you will never mind!

You're flying over the ocean, you hear your engine spit
You see your prop come to a stop, the God damn engine's quit
The ship won't float, you cannot swim, the shore is miles behind
Oh, what a dish for the crabs and fish, but you will never mind!

P-40 WARHAWK

FIGHTER

SPAN 37' 4"   LENGTH 33' 4"

*The story opposite—which might have been entitled "How I Learned to Stop Using the Gunsight for a Crutch and Start Living"—is true.
I hope the principal character is still with us!*

P-40s WERE SOMETIMES USED AS DIVE BOMBERS IN "THE BIG ONE". BLUE 3, OUR SUBJECT, SCRAMBLES FOR A CLOSE-SUPPORT MISSION —

Note: The gunsight doubled as a bombsight—when handled properly.

PULL THE ELEVATOR LOCK, CHIEF!!

TILT

NO HAND HOLD!

DURING THE BOMB RUN THE TILTED GUN-SIGHT PRODUCED A RATHER UNUSUAL FORMATION.

TALLEY HO!

MAN! AM I EVER GOIN' TO CLOBBER IT!!

DE BRIEFING

LET ME GET THIS STRAIGHT—YOU HAD 2 DIRECT HITS and ONE THREE MILES AWAY?!!

13

This page is dedicated to the grease monkeys of the AAF—those skilled technicians who were carefully taught always to use the right tool and the proper part. But the war never seemed to wait for those luxuries to catch up.

"Scrounging" parts was so commonplace that before the carcass of any aircraft cooled after a crash landing it was stripped to the bare bones by enterprising crew chiefs.

Trying to describe an airborne "clank" or "bonk" to a jaundiced crew chief after a mission was nigh on to impossible—they were a straightforward lot that must have all come from Missouri.

And nothing, but nothing, could make a crew chief madder than bringing home his airplane shot full of holes! Excuses—even through a perforated lip—fell on deaf ears.

P-38 LIGHTNING

FIGHTER

SPAN 52'   LENGTH 37'10"

THERE WAS A SHORTAGE OF PARTS...

THERE IT IS!! THAT'S THE NOISE I'VE BEEN TELLING YOU ABOUT!

IMPROVISATION WAS THE RULE...

CADET DAZE

YOU'LL GET USED TO THIS CRATE'S BACKFIRING AFTER A FEW RIDES!!

HONEST, CHIEF— I'M SORRY!

PILOT'S LAMENT

(Tune: If I Had The Wings Of An Angel)

Now listen all you pilots and you airmen
We will tell you a story sad but true
Of many who wear wings but are not happy
Gather 'round while we sing this song to you!

The many who wear wings but are not happy
Wear a smile on their lips, not in their hearts
They're overjoyed to wear the badge of an airman
But are sad in getting off to such bad starts.

A reason there must be for discontentment
Why the gloom as dark as any a blacked-out loop
Just ask them one and all and they will tell you
I'm not a member of the _____ Fighter Group!

P-47 THUNDERBOLT

FIGHTER
SPAN 40' 9"   LENGTH 36' 4"

Everyone had his own heroic ideas on skill and daring, of course, but sometimes it was tempting to see how safe you could play it . . .

THEN THERE WERE THOSE "HIGH ALTITUDE" (ABOVE 10,000') NAVIGATION TRAINING MISSIONS-

YESSIREE... WE BOMBED THOSE OL' SUB PENS TODAY FROM 5000 FEET! A MEASLY 5000!

GOR! YOU YANKS! THAT WAS BLOODY DANGEROUS!.WHY YOU COULD HAVE HIT US!

YE OLDE IRON COMPASS

BEGGIN' THE COLONEL'S PARDON! DID I PRESS THE ATTACK ON THE ME 110'S? SIR- HAVE YOU EVER TRIED TO BITE A PORCUPINE IN THE BUTT?

THERE'S THE TIME YOU LEFT THE BOMB DROP BUTTON ARMED - AND HUNG YOUR HARD HAT ON THE STICK-

(P.S. THIS LITTLE MANEUVER IS GUARANTEED TO TAKE 5 YEARS OFF YOUR LIFE)

THUD

The younger Air Force element that served in South Viet Nam may not have been aware that U. S. airmen of an earlier day were also smitten with the infectious charm of southeast Asia. Here are a few vignettes of the wartime CBI and western Pacific.

In the scene where the guy has to ask "I wonder what's on tonight?" is obviously a newcomer. After you'd been in the "boonies" a few weeks, you went to the show rain, snakes, enemy raids, etc., notwithstanding. "Abbot and Costello at the Races" was an outstanding motion picture.

Atabrine was a drug to offset the effects of that delightful malady, malaria. After taking this drug a few weeks, men have been known to turn as yellow as their Japanese adversaries. As a matter of fact, one jock flying in formation with some other P-51s over the South Pacific, was mistaken because of his yellow coloring and protruding teeth for one of the enemy and damn near got himself shot down.

The episode involving the shower actually happened to me in the Philippines. Our showers were the open air type and the local vendors wandered through while we stood there jaybird naked. The water was heated by our language at this intrusion.

IN THE CBI—IT WAS THE MONSOON...

THE PHILIPPINES...

PORTRAIT OF A TROOP WHO HAS JUST BITTEN INTO AN ATABRINE TABLET.

REMEMBER YOUR FIRST SOLO X-COUNTRY?

THE LAST BOUQUET

I've flown 'em all from then till now
The big ones and the small,
I've looped and zoomed and dove and spun
And climbed 'em to a stall,
I've flown 'em into wind and storm,
Through thunder clouds and rain
And thrilled the folks who watched me roll
My wheels along their train.

I've chased the steers across the range,
The geese from off the bay,
I've flown between the Princeton towers
When Harvard came to play,
I've clipped the wires from public poles
The blossoms from the trees
And scared my best friends half to death
With stunts far worse than these.

The rules and codes and zones they form
Are not for such as I,
Who like the great wild eagles fling
My challenge to the sky,
A bold, free spirit charging fierce
Across the fallow land —
And don't you like these nice white flowers
I'm holding in my hand?

                    Gill Robb Wilson

A-20 HAVOC

MEDIUM BOMBER
SPAN 61'4"   LENGTH 48'

Fighter jocks are a vocal lot—especially when it comes to the pros and cons of their particular steed of the moment. The "Jug", alias P-47, had many devotees, but there were a few malcontents. One thing everyone agreed on: it was big and heavy.

MAKING AN INSTRUMENT APPROACH CONSISTED OF TOSSING A BRICK OUT OVER THE RADIO CONE OF SILENCE and THEN FLYING FORMATION WITH IT —

OVERHEARD AT THE O'CLUB BAR—

OKAY, HOTSHOT! SO YOUR '51 *CAN* ACCELERATE FASTER THAN MY JUG, BUT I'LL BETCHA I CAN *OUTFALL* YA!

IT WAS ALLEGED THAT THE HEAVILY ARMORED JUG'S HIGH KILL RATIO WAS ACCOMPLISHED BY GETTING IN *FRONT* OF THE ENEMY and...

HEH, HEH, HE'LL RUN OUT OF AMMO and FUEL—*THEN* I *GOT* 'IM!

(and THERE WAS ALWAYS THE POSSIBILITY THE HUNTER MIGHT RUN INTO ONE OF HIS OWN RICOCHETS!, ED.)

LONG-RANGE ESCORT VERSIONS OF THE '47 GOT PRETTY FANCY

LOOK HOW *CALM* THEM FIGHTER PILOTS ARE!

ZAWP!

FOLD-DOWN PADDED RUDDER PEDALS

AUTO PILOT

VIBRATING SEAT

Back in those days when navaids and other essential equipment faltered, the cockpit could prove downright confining. In predicaments like these it sometimes took a mighty broad sense of humor to carry the day.

"Pathfinders" were light, or medium bombers that flew navigational lead for fighter aircraft. Most fighters had the instrument equipment equivalant to that of an early Volkswagen, e.g., just enough to let you know the engine was running. Two friends of mine (as shown in the center sequence) actually overshot our home base coming back from a mission and ended up in the drink. They were located by a B25 acting as pathfinder for another group. Suffice to say the infrequent beer ration looked exceptionally good to them that night.

The "What-the-Hell-do-I-do-now department" was another personal experience involving the pilot's relief tube. The "cup" was connected to a rubber hose located under the seat. If your seat was lowered to the bottom peg, getting the cup out could be a bit of a problem. You can imagine the bladder-busting predicament of being many miles from base with the hose stuck under the seat and just the cup in your hand.

C-46 COMMANDO

TRANSPORT-GLIDER TUG
SPAN 108'   LENGTH 76' 4"

RADIOS WERE UNPREDICTABLE

SOMETIMES BOMBERS NAVIGATED FOR THE FIGHTERS ON LONG OVERWATER HAULS.

RECIPROCALS WERE NOT UNCOMMON...

The Whathehelldoldo Now Dept.:

SITUATION: THREE HOURS OUT ON A SIX HOUR MISSION, YOU'VE CONSUMED A CANTEEN OF WATER AND HAVE JUST STRUGGLED 10 MINUTES TO GET THE RELIEF TUBE... AT LAST!

AND WHEN EVERYTHING ELSE FAILED—

MAKE ME OPERATIONS

Don't give me a P-38 with props that counter-rotate
They'll loop, roll and spin but they'll soon auger in
Don't give me a P-38!

CHORUS: Just make me Operations
Way out on some lonely atoll
For I am too young to die
I just want to go home.

Don't give me a P-39 with an engine that's mounted behind
It will tumble and roll and dig a big hole
Don't give me a P-39.

Don't give me an old Thunderbolt, it gave many pilots a jolt
It looks like a jug and it flies like a tug
Don't give me an old Thunderbolt!

Don't give me a Peter Four Oh, a hell of an airplane, I know
A ground loopin' bastard, you're sure to get plastered
Don't give me a Peter Four Oh.

Don't give me a P-51, it was alright for fighting the hun
But with coolant tank dry, you'll run out of sky
Don't give me a P-51.

Don't give me a P-61, for night flying is no fun
They say it's a lark, but I'm scared of the dark
Don't give me a P-61.

P-61 BLACK WIDOW

NIGHT FIGHTER
SPAN 66'   LENGTH 48' 11"

The subject is communications—
or the lack thereof.
Messages half received or misunderstood might
just as well have been sent by Pony Express
instead of at the speed of light . . .

WE RECEIVE A RADIO CALL IN A STAFF CAR—

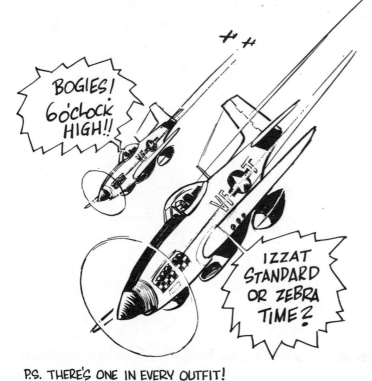

P.S. THERE'S ONE IN EVERY OUTFIT!

What makes it so strange in retrospect is that it really was that way. And the way that it was, wasn't at all the way they told you it would be before you got there. It's a good thing there wasn't too much time to think about it at the time.

Commanding officers sometimes ended up being 21 years of age and being called "the old man." The British, the Aussies, the Gurkhas, etc., etc. with their myriad of uniforms proved to be quite a problem. Our GIs often ended up saluting a corporal in his majesty's engineering corps, looking for all the world like a brigadier general with pips on his shoulders.

The two gents shown on the lower right-hand cartoon are wearing flak vests and helments —— an invention that prohibited free movement in going to the can when you really needed it.

THE OLD BOMBARDMENT GROUP

Fill that barrel up
We'll drink a loving cup
To bombers one by one
Drown your sorrow and forget tomorrow
For tomorrow never comes
Here's a health to Anti Aircraft
Here's a bumper to Pursuit, God help them
Join in all of you
We'll drink a barrel to the Old Bombardment Group.

B-24 LIBERATOR

HEAVY BOMBER
SPAN 110'   LENGTH 67' 2"

*A salute to those magnificent men in their
Liberator machines—the stalwarts who, a generation
ago, carried the air war to the enemy's doorstep—
She was big and she was heavy,
but could she ever deliver!*

THE MOST IMPORTANT PIECE OF EQUIPMENT IN THE 'LIB' WAS A EMPTY 50 CAL. AMMO BOX—

(P.S. IT WENT UNDER HERE TO KEEP THE NOSE DOWN ON THE GROUND).

CROSS SECTION OF THE BOMBARDIER AND NAVIGATOR WORKING(?) IN THE 24's SPACIOUS NOSE SECTION.

LEGEND HAS IT YOU COULD SPOT A B-24 JOCK BY HIS OVERDEVELOPED LEFT ARM (from horsin' the yoke around)!

Now it can be told .. the stirring saga of meticulous airmanship that so well served the allied cause during WW II. Above all, let us recall those skilled and painstakingly trained pilots who poured forth into combat training fields across our land.

Shown here are a few of the myriad pilot types that inhabited the U. S. air arm I've flown with every one of them and have felt like the guy in the last panel whose greatest ambition was to be able to carry the day and drink 50% alcohol and 50% grapefruit juice before it ate through the bottom of the canteen cup.

PILOT TYPES

GUNG-HO WARRIOR

EXECUTIVE TYPE

THE BUZZER

THE RATRACER:
"EH-EH-EH-EH, I GOTCHA!"

THE UNCONSCIOUS

THE SURVIVOR

AIR CORPS LAMENT

(Tune: Battle Hymn of the Republic)

Mine eyes have seen the days of men who ruled the fighting sky
With hearts that laughed at death and lived for nothing but to fly
But now those hearts are grounded and those days are long gone by
The force is shot to hell!
CHORUS: *Glory . . . flying regulations*
Have them read at every station
Crucify the man who breaks one
The force is shot to hell!

My bones have felt their pounding throb, a hundred thousand strong
A mighty airborne legion sent to right the deadly wrong
But now it's only memory, it only lives in song
The force is shot to hell!

I have seen them in their T-bolts when their eyes were dancing flame
I've seen their screaming power dives that blasted Goering's name
But now they fly like sissies and they hang their heads in shame
Their spirit's shot to hell!

They flew B-26's through a living hell of flak
And bloody, dying pilots gave their lives to bring them back
But now they all play ping pong in the operations shack
Their technique's gone to hell!

Yes, the lordly Flying Fortress and the Liberator too
Once wrote the doom of Germany with contrails in the blue
But now the skies are empty and our planes are wet with dew
And we can't fly for hell!

One day I buzzed an airfield with another happy chap
We flew a hot formation with his wingtip in my lap
But there's a new directive and we'll have no more of THAT!
Or you both will burn in Hell!

Hap Arnold built a fighting team that sang a fighting song
About the wild blue yonder in the days when men were strong
But now we're closely supervised for fear we may do wrong
The force is shot to hell!

B-17 FLYING FORTRESS

HEAVY BOMBER
SPAN 103' 9"   LENGTH 74' 4"

FINAL CHORUS: Glory! No more regulations!
Rip them down at every station!
Ground the guy that tries to make one!
AND LET US FLY LIKE HELL!

Some men who drive weapon-laden airplanes with utter nonchalance get a little sweaty-palmed when handed a loaded pistol. Even a flare gun earns a certain respect. On the other hand, the darn thing might not have even been loaded . . .

There you were -- clean cut, a true-blue intrepid co-pilot. Under the direction, of course, of the pilot. You wanted to fly that bird so what happened? Nothing! Might as well have been in the Quartermaster Corps for all the chance the old buzzard gave you to take the wheel.

This sequence really doesn't need any prose. It's dedicated to all of those silent warriors who sat hour after hour glued to the right seat while some old walrus glommed onto the controls. You just sat there boring holes in the air hour after hour without a peep.

PV-2 HARPOON

MEDIUM BOMBER
SPAN 75'   LENGTH 52'

THE COPILOT

I'VE GOT SIXPENCE

I've got sixpence
Jolly, jolly sixpence
I've got sixpence to last me all my life
I've got twopence to spend
And twopence to lend
And twopence to send home to my wife—poor wife.

CHORUS: No cares have I to grieve me
No pretty little girls to deceive me
I'm happy as a lark believe me
As we go rolling, rolling home
Rolling home (rolling home)
Rolling home (rolling home)
By the light of the silvery mo-ooon
Happy is the day when the airman gets his pay
As we go rolling, rolling home.

I've got fourpence
Jolly, jolly fourpence
I've got fourpence to last me all my life
I've got twopence to spend
And twopence to lend
And no pence to send home to my wife—poor wife.

I've got twopence
Jolly, jolly twopence
I've got twopence to last me all my life
I've got twopence to spend
And no pence to lend
And no pence to send home to my wife—poor wife.

I've got no pence
Jolly, jolly no pence
I've got no pence to last me all my life
I've got no pence to spend
And no pence to lend
And no pence to send home to my wife—poor wife.

A-26 INVADER

MEDIUM BOMBER
SPAN 70'   LENGTH 49' 11"

*Now that the majority of us winged warriors
of World War II are sprouting gray hairs
among the gold, this meander down memory lane
may serve to help conjure up those splendid
days of our bygone youth . . .*

REMEMBER?

- **T**HOSE 'PARACHUTE BAGS' LOADED WITH EVERYTHING BUT A PARACHUTE YOU TOOK WITH YOU PCS, TDY TDN, ETC., ETC.

... AND THOSE SHEEPSKIN FLYING DUDS, (USUALLY ISSUED IN THE TROPICS)

KASPRONG! (SOUND OF A HERNIA)

- **T**HAT GREAT WARTIME BOOZE MADE OF '100% NATURAL **CANE** SPIRITS'?

OLD PANTHER POOP

THIS STUFF'D BLOW A SAFE!

- **T**RYING TO HIT THE JOHN IN THE BACK OF A GOONEY-BIRD IN ROUGH AIR?

- **T**ROPICAL 'BUTTER' THAT REFUSED TO MELT? (IT JUST SHRIVELLED UP AND TURNED BLACK!)

SPUT

CRACKLE

- **H**AVING 84 POINTS IN AN AREA WITH 85 POINTS FOR ROTATION ??

- **T**HE 'RUPTURED DUCK' LAPEL PIN?

Looking back, you get that *I wouldn't go through it again for a million bucks but it was a great experience* feeling. But when you were ready for rotation there was one primary emotion...with maybe a twinge of nostalgia for the old air mattress and a condescending regard for your replacement.

In days when canned meat was very precious back home and it took a full book of ration stamps to buy it, my folks saved up stamps for several months and sent me canned Spam at a time when I couldn't look another tin of the stuff in the eye (Spam was the only meat entree for most air force troops in the Pacific).

By longevity and just "out-livin' 'em" you accrued such niceties as air matresses and Primis stoves from those who had gone before. When it came time to go home, these precious items were very carefully rationed to the next senior in line. I'll never forget the time I was overdue getting back to the base and got there just in time to find my sleeping bag, flying boots and air mattress being claimed by my recently "bereaved" friends.

I WANTED WINGS

I wanted wings 'til I got the God damn things
Now I don't want them any more
They taught me how to fly, then they sent me here to die
I've got a belly full of war
You can save those Zeros for the other God damn heroes
For distinguished flying crosses do not compensate for losses.

CHORUS: I wanted wings 'til I got the God damn things
                Now I don't want them any more.

I'll take the dames while the rest go down in flames
I've no desire to be burned
Air combat's no romance and it made me wet my pants
I'm not a fighter, I have learned
You can leave the Mitsubishes for the crazy sons-a-bitches
'Cause I'd rather lay a woman than be picked up by a Grumman.

I'm too young to die in a God damn PBY
That's for the eager, not for me.
I won't trust to luck to be picked up in a "Duck"
After I've crashed into the sea.
I would rather be a bellhop than a flier on a flattop
With my hand around a bottle not a God damn throttle.

I don't want to tour over Berlin or the Ruhr
Ack Ack always makes me lose my lunch
For me there's no Hey Hey when they holler "Bombs Away"!
I'd rather be at home with the bunch
For there's one thing you can't laugh off
And that's when they shoot your ass off
And I'd rather be home, Buster, with my ass than with a cluster.

They feed us lousy chow, but we stay alive somehow
On dehydrated eggs and milk and stew
The rumor has it next they'll be dehydrating sex
And that's the day I'll tell the coach I'm through
For I've managed all the dangers, the shooting back of strangers
But when I get home late I want my woman straight, Buster.

PEGGY

MEDIUM BOMBER

Whether apprehensive or devil-may-care, any warrior on duty in the darkness of night might well appreciate these words from Shakespeare's King Lear: "Things that love night / love not such nights as these. The wrathful skies / Gallow the very wanderers of the dark / And make them keep their caves."

A SENTRY POST ON A FLIGHT LINE IN WW II –

* sound of a rifle bolt sliding home

THIS HAS GOT TO BE ONE OF THE HOARIEST LEGENDS IN THE AIR FORCE.
SITUATION: TWO CADETS ON A NIGHT CROSS COUNTRY.

Stateside duty was sometimes hard to take . . . when you'd already done an overseas tour. It was training, training and more training. Of course, there were occasional forays into the nearby villages to fraternize with the friendly natives.

A rerun of WW II would not be complete without a look into the aviation cadet training program. The wayward cadet was given "gigs." One gig amounted to one hour of marching. Now marching at any time, notwithstanding the fact that you might have to carry a rifle, or wear a parachute while doing same, was very, very detrimental to the morale of birdmen. I had one friend that had so many gigs that when he transferred from station to station they followed him on his record like the plague and he was still walking tours up to the point when they called him up to get his commission. Chicken? You bet.

And there isn't an insurance company in the world that would insure you as a tow pilot on a cadet gunnery range.

C-54 SKYMASTER

TRANSPORT
SPAN 117' 6"   LENGTH 93' 10"

THE 'COMPLEAT' AVIATOR
circa 1944

EQUIPMENT FOR ENTERING A DIVE~

DANNY'S DIVE

CAP, 50 MISSION, CRUSH, TYPE 44. (IT HELPED IF YOU SLEPT ON IT)

WINGS, SHINY (ANY TYPE WOULD DO)

GLASSES, DARK. (ONE-WAY TYPE BEST)

RIBBONS, MOLDY

BRACELET, "CRASH"

WATCH, HACK, M-1 THE BIGGER THE FACE, THE BETTER.

WALLET, MONEY (AND LOTS OF IT BROTHER!)

50 GIRLS 50

PINKS, SLIGHTLY CREASED

BOOTS, FLYING. (NOTE CASUAL, BUT REVEALING DRAPE OF TROUSERS)

SIR! HOW MANY POINTS DO I GET FOR THE TOWSHIP?

NOW THAT'S WHAT I CALL WALKING OFF A LOT OF GIGS!

OKAY MEN! WE'RE APPROACHING THE BASE. PULL IT UP! - LET'S MAKE IT LOOK GOOD!

"PULL IT UP!" HELL! I'VE GOT EVERY-THING OPEN BUT THE TOOL BOX, NOW!

CLANK BONK!

HERE'S TO THE REGULAR AIR FORCE

(Tune: My Bonnie Lies Over the Ocean)

In peace time the regulars are happy
In peace time they're happy to serve
But let them get into a fracas
And they'll call out the God damn reserves!

CHORUS: Call out, call out
        Call out the God damn reserves, reserves!
        Call out, call out
        Oh, call out the God damn reserves.

Here's to the Regular Air Force
They have such a wonderful plan
They call up the God damn reservist
Whenever the shit hits the fan!

They call up every old pilot
They call up every young man
The reservists they go to Korea
The regulars stay in Japan!

Here's to the Regular Air Force
With medals and badges galore
If it weren't for the God damn reservists
Their ass would be draggin' the floor!

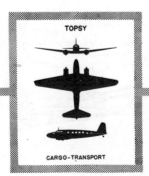

TOPSY

CARGO-TRANSPORT

The story opposite is true. Only the names have been omitted—to protect the book from lawsuit. I won't say who the star of the show was—all I'll admit to is, "There I Was . . ."

The unbounded glee of acceptance as a cadet . . . arrival of the flight at the flight training center . . . humiliation at the hands of those infallible upperclassmen . . . and finally, that indescribable moment of your first solo. Training planes were very cleverly designed with a one-way communication system -- to cadet. This made for lots of one-sided conversations.

However, we "gadgets" had some retribution. To get a nervous instructor (some became paranoid after a few months teaching) into a tight formation while we see-sawed back and forth over his head with our wing tips provided some revenge for all of the brow beating we took on that intercom.

The terror -- and the delight -- of your first solo is best portrayed by the guy in the center of the page who figures today can't be the day, can it?

SBD DAUNTLESS

DIVE BOMBER

SPAN 41' 6"   LENGTH 32' 6"

(AND THERE WAS NO WAY TO TURN HIM OFF, EITHER)

ME--SOLO--TODAY?

When jets first came on the scene, a new book had to be written. The sequences depicted opposite were attributed to a 2d Lt. Bruce Jones. Bruce developed the "Selfridge Let-down" long before anyone ever heard of a "teardrop" jet instrument approach pattern . . .

ONE HAND ON THE THROTTLE

One hand on the throttle
One hand on the throttle
One hand on the bottle
One hand on the bottle
Both feet in my pockets
Both feet in my pockets
Off we go into the wild blue yonder
. . . . . . CRASH!

HELEN

MEDIUM BOMBER

Instructors who live and keep their sanity
Are often lacking in urbanity.
The student—duller than a hoe—
Is the guy who makes it so . . .

SCENE: INSTRUMENT FLIGHT CHECK WITH A PARTICULARLY SNOTTY INSTRUCTOR—

SCENE: A PRIMARY JET TRAINING BASE; A DUAL RIDE, INSTRUCTOR TO NEW T-37* STUDENT TAXIING OUT FOR TAKEOFF:

* AFFECTIONATELY CALLED THE 'TWEETY-BIRD' OR 'CONVERTER' (CONVERTS FUEL INTO NOISE)

It has been said that the business of flying can best be described as hour and hours of boredom -- interspersed with moments of stark terror. On the next couple of pages, you'll find some of the moments of stark terror that have occurred to me in 25 years of flying.

The gear-up landing sequence reminds me of the story of the guy who testified before the accident board that he couldn't hear the tower's warning that his gear was not down because of the loud blowing of a horn in his ear.

When the air gets cluttered with other birds, a flyspeck on a windshield can double your heartbeat.

F7F TIGER CAT

FIGHTER

SPAN 51' 6" LENGTH 45' 5"

Random Moments of Terror

THE DROPPED FLASHLIGHT BIT:

THE "WHAT-THE-HELL-IS-THAT-HORN?" DRAMA:

THE "NEAR MISS" EXPERIENCE:

HERE'S TO _____

Here's to _____, he's true blue
He's a drunkard through and through
He's a drunkard so they say
Oh, he might go to heaven but he went the other way
So drink chug-a-lug, chug-a-lug, chug-a-lug
So drink chug-a-lug, chug-a-lug, chug-a-lug.

TABBY

CARGO-TRANSPORT

The good, the bad, the droll, the sad
Add up to war's perdition.
For airmen, long-of-tooth or young,
They're part of our tradition . . .

Remember **GREMLINS?** Inherited from the RAF (1928). There were good ones, bad ones, mischievous ones — they all had one thing in common: "They were the little men who usually were not there"—

(THE LANDING GEAR THAT WASN'T)

Another ubiquitous group during WW II (and in Korea and Vietnam, too!) was the U.S.O.- God bless 'em!

And will you ever forget *these* characters?...

KILROY

thanks to Sgt. Geo. Baker

in memory of Lt. Dave Breger

Breathes there a pilot whose heart hath ne'er turned flip-flops over some untoward occurrance during the swift completion of his appointed rounds? My CO and I lost a fan on a B25 one day right after take off -- this prompted the sequence shown at the top of the page. Yep, you're right -- we started to feather the wrong one. An alert flight engineer saved us from a rice paddy. In getting it unfeathered, we nearly tore the skin off each other's hands working the knobs and dials.

I was a flying safety officer for many years, and almost every conceivable type of excuse has been given for why you picked up clothesline or an outhouse door on a wing tip when you were supposed to be flying a reconnaissance mission at 30,000 feet.

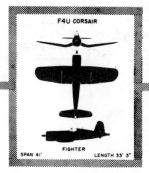

F4U CORSAIR

FIGHTER
SPAN 41'   LENGTH 33' 3"

THE ENGINE-FAILURE TRAUMA:

QUICK! FEATHER NO. 1 WE'VE BLOWN A JUG!

BLAM!
BONK!

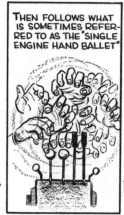

THEN FOLLOWS WHAT IS SOMETIMES REFERRED TO AS THE "SINGLE ENGINE HAND BALLET"

GUESS WHICH ONE YOU FEATHERED AL, GUESS!!

THE "I-DIDN'T-KNOW-IT-WAS-BELOW-MINIMUMS" APPROACH:

CRIPES! WHAT LOUSY WEATHER! THE BIRDS MUST BE WALKIN'! THERE'S SOMETHING AHEAD -- MUST BE THE RUNWAY!

①

NOW, TELL ME AGAIN - WHAT WAS THE FIRST THING YOU SAW? ...

②

SEARS

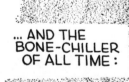

... AND THE BONE-CHILLER OF ALL TIME:

Bandits! 6 o'clock high!

THE HANDSOME YOUNG AIRMAN

A handsome young airman lay dying
And as on the airdrome he lay
To mechanics who 'round him came sighing
These last parting words he did say:
"Take the cylinders out of my kidneys,
The connecting rods out of my brain,
The crank-shaft out of my backbone
And assemble the engine again."

SONIA

DIVE BOMBER

"The time has come," the artist said,
"To speak of many things . . .
The ups and downs of flying clowns,
And cannons wearing wings."

ROGER RUDDER

- PILOT EXTRAORDINAIRE
- BON VIVANT!
- ALL-ROUND GOOD FELLOW
- *and* EXPENDABLE!
(BEING A SECOND LOOEY)

ROG IS DEMONSTRATING A SLOW ROLL TO A CADET

⊚!*!⊚
Fell out of it! Boy! am I ever *screwed up!*
* ⊚!
←OVER R/T *NOT* INTERCOM

-- AND FROM THE TOWER--

Aircraft that just made a transmission! Give the tower your call sign!!

LISSEN BUSTER, I'M NOT *THAT* SCREWED UP!!!

GENERAL GEORGE KENNEY'S WARRIORS IN 5TH AIR FORCE RIGGED UP A *75 MM* CANNON IN A B-25....IT WAS A REAL RIVET POPPER! ACTUALLY IT COULD FIRE QUITE RAPIDLY AND MADE ONE HELLOFA STRAFING WEAPON!!

Man! that's what I call recoil!!

BARROOM!

NORTH AMERICAN BUILT MORE THAN 1400 OF THESE BIRDS (the 'G'&'H')

Aviatrix Jacqueline Cochran banded together a group of women pilots to form the Women's Auxiliary Service Pilots (WASP). And, brother, some of them could sting like their namesakes. I'll never forget trying to get one to move over on a pilot lounge seat to make room for some other weary pilots. (She was stretched out full length.) She used some very un-teaparty-like language in telling me where to go!

By and large (no pun intended) they were a game lot and did a lot of the "garbage" flying; slow-timing engines, maintenance test hops, ferrying etc.

Some of the gals were checked out in "hotter" aircraft than their male counterparts. We had them at a real disadvantage, though, because all of the "facilities" were designed for John pilot -- not Joan.

A BASIC FLYING SCHOOL — 1943

A 38!! MAN! LOOK AT THAT HOT PILOT!

YEH! LET'S GO MEET HIM AT BASE OPS!

AND THEN

HIYA *BOYS!*

CADETS WHO THOUGHT FLYING WAS SOLELY A HE-MAN'S PROFESSION

THESE GAME GALS OFTEN SLOW-TIMED BIRDS...
THIS ONE MADE ONE HELLOFA HARD LANDING
IN THE OL' JUG...

HER REPORT:

BOTH WINGS TOO HEAVY.
Mary Jones

THERE WERE BOUND TO BE SOME MISTAKES—

HEY FATSO! PUTTIN' A LITTLE LARD ON THE UNDERCARRIAGE AREN'T YA?

WHAT'S IT TO YOU, BUSTER?!

BARNACLE BILL THE PILOT

(Tune: Barnacle Bill the Sailor)

The Air Corps is the life for me, said Barnacle Bill the Sailor
I'll jump my ship and leave the sea and be an aviator
I'll fly so high I'll reach the sky, gravitation I'll defy
I'll make the people moan and cry, said Barnacle Bill the Sailor.

    Pretty soon you'll lose that grin, said the fair young maiden
    Pretty soon you'll lose that grin, said the fair young maiden

I'm rough and tough, I know my stuff, said Bill the aviator
I'll fly this ship till I've had enough, said Bill the aviator
I know a strut, I know a fin, I know a barrel-roll and a spin
I know a prop, I know a stick, and I know an elevator.

    You're out of gas and must go down, wailed the fair young maiden
    You're out of gas and must go down, wailed the fair young maiden

I'm a cockeyed Finn if I'll give in, roared Bill the aviator
I'll fight this ship with a flyer's grin, roared Bill the aviator
He kicked the bar and pulled the stick, which didn't seem to do the trick
And he hit the ground like a ton of brick, poor Barnacle Bill the Sailor.

    Here's some flowers for his grave, sobbed the fair young maiden
    Here's some flowers for his grave, sobbed the fair young maiden

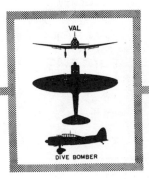

Retractable landing gear added a new dimension to flying—more speed, more maneuverability, more things to forget. When they first appeared, belly landings were as common as that ol' Air Force saying: "I couldn't hear the tower because of that horn blowin' in my ear!"

To paraphrase a Churchillian saying, never was so little known by so many about so much . . . but we learned, luv, we learned. Oh, how we learned.

All of those pamphlets they gave you about the exotic foreign lands you were to visit never quite filled the bill. Phrases like "how do I lead my horse to water" just didn't seem to cut it when you were "on the economy."

England was a foreign land to us and after listening to some of the Cockney, there was no question about being in an alien environment. All that can be remembered between missions was the fog, leaky nissen huts (the poor man's version of a quonset hut), the fact that everyone was in uniform and that the pubs dispensed not only beer but warmth and friendship for lonely Americans.

F6F HELLCAT

FIGHTER
SPAN 42' 10"   LENGTH 33' 4"

ENGLAND, circa 1943, we had an L-of-a lot of experiences:

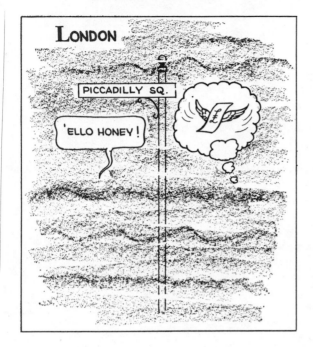

LONDON

PICCADILLY SQ.

'ELLO HONEY!

LEAKING NISSEN HUTS

ROGER, THESE MUST BE THOSE "CRISP FALL DAYS" THIS RUDDY GI PAMPHLET TALKS ABOUT!

LAND ARMY GIRLS

SAY CHOLLIE, HAVE YA HEARD ABOUT THAT NEW BRITISH TANK?

'LIMEYS'

GIMME AN 'ARF N' ARF LUV!

GUINNESS IS GOOD FOR YOU!

"FOREIGN WORDS AND PHRASES"

THE LADY IN RED

'Twas a cold winter's evening
The guests were all leaving
O'Leary was closing the bar
When he turned and he said to the lady in red
"Get out, you can't stay where you are."
She wept a sad tear in her bucket of beer
And she thought of the cold night ahead
When a gentleman dapper stepped out of the crapper
And these are the words that he said:

"Her mother never told her
The things a young girl should know
About the ways of Air Force men
And how they come and go—mostly go
Now age has taken her beauty
And sin has left its sad scar
So remember your mothers and sisters, boys
And let her sleep under the bar."

C-54 SKYMASTER

TRANSPORT

While all airmen perforce belong to that elite brotherhood of the noble, a heroic stance is difficult to maintain once the winds of adversity begin to blow, and you find yourself shot down in flames—or in conversation . . .

THE SQUADRON HOTSHOT (EVERY OUTFIT'S GOT AT LEAST ONE) IS MOUTHING OFF—

DO *I* KNOW THE GEN?! WHY JUST THIS MORNING WE HAD A TALK --

I WAS ON THE RAMP WHEN HE STARTED HIS '17 AND HE SAID TO ME..

"PULL THE *6!☼!6 CHOCKS, STUPID*!?*"

YOU DIDN'T - PER CHANCE - HAPPEN TO BRING AN EXTRA TOOTHBRUSH ALONG DID YOU?

INSTRUMENT INSTRUCTORS COULD BE PARTICULARLY SARCASTIC—

(UNDER THE HOOD)

BE*OOT*IFUL RECOVERY MISTER!

"I tell you -- it was hell on the home front! I was so scrogged up by the end of my delay en route in the ZI that it was a pleasure to get back to the combat theater. In fact, when I arrived in England I put out a service star for my mother back in Poughkeepsie . . ." so goes a World War II ditty about a pilot on leave in the states.

Another WW II saga about a returning war hero pilot was the bawdy record entitled "Roger Rudder." AAF folklore has it that this recording was made by a gaggle of troops just returned from the Pacific. They cut it while ensconced in a San Francisco hotel, well plied with the juice of the grape. The story deals with a Roger Rudder -- a hot-shot second looey who returns home with a rather jaundiced eye and a chip on his shoulder for "all those 4 f's." The language used in the record -- which is a collectors' item and pretty hard to find -- couldn't be used in this book, however some of the "sanitized" highlights of Roger's comments upon returning to the zone of interior are shown on the opposite page. He kept a fulltime PIO officer busy trying to clean up Rog's right-to-the-point messages for the home folks.

Part of many returns aces' duties involved the selling of war bonds and there's many a jock who would rather face 14 Zeros than stand on a platform and deliver a discourse on how he became a hero.

A-26 INVADER

MEDIUM BOMBER
SPAN 70'   LENGTH 49' 11"

I'VE GOT THE CLANKS

(Tune: You're Just in Love)

I hear vectors when the sky is clear
I see bogies when there's no one near
I get clanky when I'm in the sky
Way up so high
On GCI.

I get shaky when I'm in the soup
Think I'll transfer back into the Group
Red lights in the cockpit of the Deuce
Are out to clobber me
I've got the clanks.

We don't need supervision
We don't need T.O. revision
We don't need directives from the Group
We all know what's the matter
We just get a bunch of chatter
When we try to get the latest poop.

Colonel _____ has no feeling,
His letters are not revealing
Never says if he's pleased or not
There is nothing he can buy
To help me when I'm in the sky
'Cause I'm not brave, I've got the clanks.

C-47 SKYTRAIN

TRANSPORT-GLIDER TUG

Back in the days when not all airmen were all-airman, riding shotgun in a C-45 could be a good way to catch up on your sleep. But sometimes it called for ambassadorial self-control . . .

71

Bouncing along over Europe in a late model B17 flying fort or a B24 Liberator on air highways paved with flak while friendly and bogie fighters played tag through the formations led one to wonder if this trip was really necessary.

Radio silence on a mission was the order of the day. However, in the "exuberance" of meeting the enemy, this was not strictly enforced. The most famous intercom exchange that I can recall went something like this: First voice: "Who dat?" Second voice: "Who dat say who dat?" Third voice: "Who dat say who dat say who dat?" Fourth voice (Wing Commander): "Knock it off!" First voice: "Who dat?" . . . ad nauseum.

B-17 FLYING FORTRESS

HEAVY BOMBER

SPAN 103' 9"   LENGTH 74' 4"

THE AIR OVER EUROPE COULD GET PRETTY CLUTTERED AT TIMES:

C'MON DOWN - I'VE GOT 6 JERRIES CORNERED OVER HERE!!

THE "GATHERING OF THE CLAN" AT A TYPICAL BRITISH BUNCHER BEACON.

THE UNSEEN AUDIENCE -

TABLE SONG

This is table number one
Number one, number one
This is table number one
Where in the hell is two?

This is table (Squadron number)
Who in the hell are you?

This is table best of all
Best of all, best of all
This is table best of all
Who in the hell are you?

PV-2 HARPOON

MEDIUM BOMBER

We trained and we trained and we trained, and we knew the gadgets and the gimmicks cold. Or that's what we thought when we got our wings. But somehow, in the cold reality of flight, not everything came up roses . . .

IT'S A DARK AND STORMY NIGHT-LOTSA LIGHTNING...

...AND AT GROUND LEVEL, PANIC REIGNS SUPREME...

AND THEN THERE'S THE CLOWN WHO PULLS BACK THE STICKGRIP TO MAKE HIS ENGINE RUNUP--HAVING LEFT HIS GUN SWITCH ON 'ARM'.

We tried to keep soul and sinew together in a military manner, but all those different types you find in an army unnerved us with their separate styles which were unique and sometimes insane. But somehow we managed -- somehow.

It never failed that after an intricate and detailed briefing some idiot would always ask for a repeat. When your nerves are raw and on edge over the impending mission, a question like "How's that again?" are grounds for justifiable homicide.

The A20 and A26 attack bombers flew missions so low that they had to gain altitude to get back in the traffic pattern. Navigation became a real problem unless you could read French and German and take the signs off the train stations as you went by.

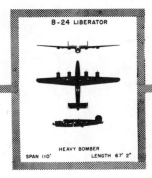

*ALLIED EXPEDITIONARY AIR FORCE (FREE FRENCH)

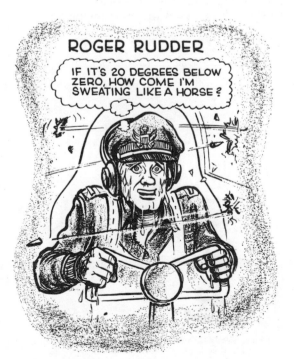

IT'S A SHYME

We were comfy back in England
Drinking beer and ale and wine
When they slipped it to us, greasy
And shipped us out to the front line.

CHORUS: It's a shyme the 'ole world over
It's a shyme around the map
The civilians gets the gravy
While the Air Force gets the crap.

Now we were young and we were eager
Ten more missions and we're 'ome
But they goosed us without warning
Sent us flying 'cross the foam.

As we flew over Windsor Castle
And saluted all the 'ores
We got it up the arse'ole
And we're far from Britain's shores.

So we fly our stinking aircraft
And we're risking all our lives
While the cruds wot gyve us orders
Are shacking with our wives.

So as you sit amidst your family
Blessed be the tie that binds
Say a prayer for the Air Force
Wot got it rammed up their behinds.

PV-1 VENTURA

MEDIUM BOMBER

Here's to the chaplains, God bless 'em. The best of them spent a lot of time on the line and in the air. They knew when to talk, when to listen . . . and when not to listen . . .

79

Even as far back as the latter days of World War II, the jet age, with a little age of automation thrown in, was beginning to force itself on the good old "seat of the pants" hotshots. The effect was bewildering. Some still haven't got over it.

There's a story of a P51 jock who -- with everything open but the tool box -- roared across southern Europe chasing one of the new German jets. (He ran himself out of fuel and was captured.) The Luftwaffe's rocket ships had a blinding rate-of-climb. An airplane that could fly vertically through your formation was very disturbing.

"V" mail (to save space) seemed to be written on the back side of a postage stamp. It did save space but increased the volume of mail -- you had to follow it up with regular sized letters explaining what you said in the first one.

Re Roger Rudder, if you've ever been upside down in an airplane you'll soon discover that things that normally slosh about in the bottom of the machine suddenly obscure your vision.

P-61 BLACK WIDOW
NIGHT FIGHTER
SPAN 66'   LENGTH 48' 11"

THERE ARE A FEW GUYS AROUND WHO'LL REMEMBER — WITH CONSIDERABLE TRAUMA — WHEN THE JERRIES USHERED IN THE JET & ROCKET ERA:

FRIG THE FLYING FORTRESS

A navigator sits in front
Surrounded by his maps
He belches in the intercom
And wakes us from our naps.

CHORUS: Frig the flying fortress
And pray that she'll abort
We'd rather be at home than in
The friggin' flyin' fort.

The captain sits upon the left
He flys the fort with ease
But he hands it to the co-pilot
When we're heading for the trees.

The midway gunner has to stand
To give his guns a pull
But that's alright 'cause in the fight
His hands get mighty full.

Then pity the poor tail gunner for
His space is very sparce
And when the landing gear retracts
He gets it up the arse.

Well, radio operator passed
On the news report
He says that congress just outlawed
The friggin' flying' fort.

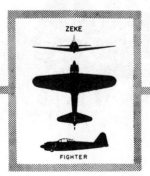

It was 1944 and our magnificent men and their flying machines were locked in a gargantuan struggle to restore peace to a world in flames. But even in the midst of the holocaust, it was the minor problems one dealt with every day that kept things interesting.

Fighter jocks were always telling the bomber crews what a soft deal bomber duty was -- just sitting there driving in a straight line with all those engines, with all those guns, with all those fighters to protect you. But as any bomber man will tell you, it wasn't all that easy.

Actually, the camaraderie between the bomber and fighter people was very close. One of the loneliest feelings in the world as a bomber crew was to watch your fighter escort turn and head back to Jolly Old due to the "little friends" limited fuel. Later, fighters got bigger tanks and went the whole butt-numbing distance.

I'll admit that the guy hanging out of the nose wheelwell as a jury-rigged wheel is stretching it a bit. However, many a crew chief or flight engineer "rinky-dinked" equipment in order to bring your bird home. Tape, wire, string and sometimes even urine in the shot-up hydraulic system would carry the day.

In the Roger Rudder sequence, it never failed -- just as soon as you crossed the bomb line the "urge" struck you and never let up until you crossed it again homeward bound.

A-20 HAVOC

MEDIUM BOMBER
SPAN 61'4"   LENGTH 48'

ROGER RUDDER

OLD SOLDIERS NEVER DIE

Old soldiers never die, never die, never die
Old soldiers never die, they just fade away.
Old sailors never buy, never buy, never buy
Old sailors never buy, they just sail away.
Old pilots never fly, never fly, never fly
Old pilots never fly, they just draw their pay.

The tributaries feeding into the
generation gap are the terminology
chasm and the credibility canyon.
In any case, old and bold flyers are
certain to recognize old and bold liars . . .

ROGER RUDDER

The crew chief's idea of heaven must be the air force museum where airplanes are polished to perfection and never flown again. But then, what else could match the pride he felt in pasting another meatball or swastika on the cockpit of his personal instrument of war, which was occasionally loaned out to some thoughtless pilot.

3 HOURS LATER

WILL YOU GO BOOM TODAY?

(Tune: Ta-Ra-Ra Boom-Der-E)

If you fly an 89
You must be deaf, dumb and blind
For your life ain't worth a dime
What's your scheduled blow-up time?

CHORUS: Will you go boom today?
          Will you go boom today?
          Two blew up yesterday
          We haven't lost a day.

If you fly an 86
You'll have wings like broken sticks
Suddenly you'll see a glare
You'll be pieces everywhere.

If you fly an 84
You may have a perfect score
Ten times up and ten times down
Bang! And you go underground.

If you fly a 94
You will never holler more
For your lot we don't pine
It's better than an 89.

If you fly a 102
Don't go up unless it's blue
For if it feels one drop of rain
You'll have wreckage, not a plane.

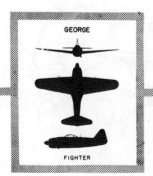

GEORGE

FIGHTER

Flexible planning is a virtue often practiced in inverse ratio to one's distance from the problem. But how marvelously the mind concentrates on alternatives when the planner's own anatomy is in the well-known sling!

Decisions were always difficult in war time. There were times when you didn't know what to do and many, many more times when nothing you did was right.

Feathering an engine on a bird with multi-fans over enemy territory was tantamount to painting a target on your behind. Enemy fighters had a field day with cripples.

As the allied air forces moved into Europe after D-Day the spoils of war grew at a phenomenal rate and it took an extra truck or two to carry the poker stakes.

Roger Rudder demonstrates the old axiom that there are no atheists in foxholes -- whether they be on the ground or at 20,000 feet.

REMEMBER THOSE CRAZY SIGNPOSTS?

ROGER RUDDER

FLAK SHOWERS

(Tune: April Showers)

Although flak showers may come your way
They'll bring the panic, that makes you say:
"My fuel is Josephine, I'm going home
So if you want to stay and fight, you may
Stay and fight alone!
I've added throttle, I'm on my way
I'll live to come back some other day
So keep on strafing that position
And knock it out for me
I'm just a close supporter, can't you see!"

FRANK

FIGHTER

When fighter jocks misread their clocks
And don't fire on the hour,
It gives this dude disquietude—
And super pucker power.

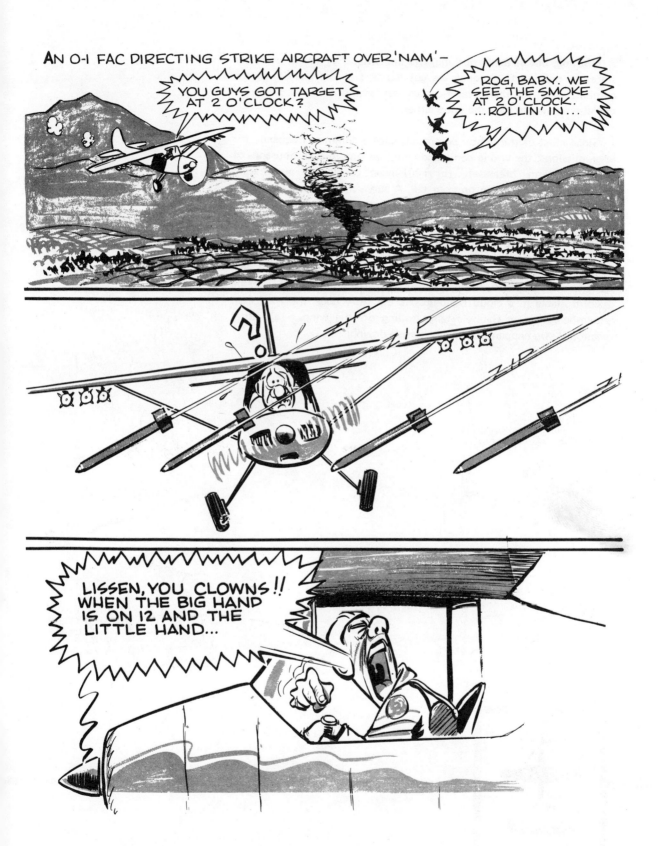

Nothing, but virtually nothing, was like what they taugnt us at our stateside training fields once we got exposed to the realities of the combat zone. But there was a certain satisfaction in knowing that no one else seemed to have the poop either.

Since most of the fighter commands used a common frequency for large missions, the wrong command could be transmitted thousands of miles. The term "break left" (or right) meant usually just one thing -- somebody was boring in on your tail. A survival reaction was to drop your external fuel tanks before closing with the enemy. At one point, I guess our allied ground forces could have walked across Europe on the drop tanks that were flung from "breaking" fighters.

Speaking about drop tanks, it is alleged that the war's leading ace, Col. Gabby Gabreski, had to bail out after his aircraft became uncontrollable in a cloud build-up. As the story goes, the wing man remembered seeing Gabby's tanks rolling off the wings -- a natural reaction if you happen to be flying upside down.

P-51 MUSTANG

FIGHTER

SPAN 37'   LENGTH 32' 3"

AH! THOSE ENGLISH MORNS!

RED LEADER, HOW'S THE VISIBILITY? CAN YOU SEE THE LIGHTS?

SEE THE *LIGHTS!* HELL, I CAN'T EVEN SEE MY COPILOT!

HEY MAC, WHERE'S THE LATRINE?

YER STANDIN' IN IT, JACK!

(MAN, OH MAN! THOSE BLACKOUTS)

SURE WAY TO WIN A POPULARITY POLL IN A DEBRIEFING--

AND SO ON ACROSS EUROPE.

BREAK LEFT!

OOPS! I MEAN BLINDMAN FLIGHT 'BREAK LEFT'

WE HAD A LOT TO LEARN ABOUT INSTRUMENT FLYING—

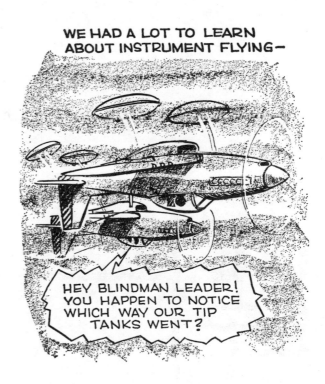

HEY BLINDMAN LEADER! YOU HAPPEN TO NOTICE WHICH WAY OUR TIP TANKS WENT?

A NAVY PRAYER

Our father who art in Washington
Truman is thy name
The Navy's done
The Air Force won
On the Atlantic as in the Pacific
Give us this day our appropriation
And forgive us our accusations
As we forgive our accusers
Lead us not into temptation
But deliver us from Matthews and Johnson
For thine is the power
The B-36 and the Air Force
Forever and ever - Airmen.

JUDY 33

DIVE BOMBER

Engines and airframes and armaments change,
As do ceilings and airspeeds and ferry range,
But what keeps 'em flying—according to rumor—
Is the airman's kind of wild-blue humor.

'FREDDY THE FAC'

Of course, the USO came out our way whenever they could. But for the most part in those tropic climates we created our own diversions and through it all there was that ever present spirit of camaraderie marred only occasionally by little spurts of hysteria.

A backfiring engine in mid-Pacific could make the cockpit the most popular place around. A sure way to terminate a nap.

The lads in the lower left hand corner are doing their bit for the psyshological warfare department, an outfit dedicated to burying the enemy under leaflets.

PB4Y-2 PRIVATEER

PATROL BOMBER
SPAN 110'   LENGTH 74' 7"

THE INVADER

Oh, the Invader is a very fine airplane
Constructed of steel and tin
It will do over three hundred level
The plane with the tailwind built in!
Oh, why did I join the Air Force
Mother, dear Mother knew best
For here I lie in the wreckage
Invader all over my chest!

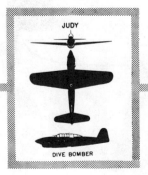

If at first you don't succeed, try, try again.
Disregard the small arms:
Thanks to you, whom we admire,
Those cotton-pickin' fighter jocks will fly, fly again.

A DOWNED FIGHTER JOCK IS BEING SCARFED UP BY A JOLLY GREEN IN 'NAM—

WE'RE HIT! ...LOSING POWER!

CRUMP!

ANOTHER CHOPPER SWOOPS IN—

OKAY, RESCUE CONTROL! WE GOT THE CREW OF THE LOW BIRD AND THE FIGHTER JOCK!

THIS CHOPPER IS A DIFFERENT RIDE THAN THE '105, ISN'T IT, SIR?

IT'S NOT THE RIDE I MIND, SON, IT'S THE *TRANSFERS* THAT ARE KILLIN' ME!

In his dispensary tent the doc could be heartless when all you wanted was a little extra sack time or a dash of medicinal spirits. But when he ventured out of his office into yours, he occasionally revealed more human tendencies.

Some of the best friends I had in the second unpleasantness were flight surgeons -- a truly dedicated lot. It seems strange, but most of them were obstetricians. Now you can't get any further from your training than assignments like that! Medicinal alcohol was 190 proof and it would evaporate if you left the cap off. The only way you could get it past your tongue was to cut it 50-50 with G.I. grapefruit juice. This mixture -- it is rumored -- was primarily responsible for the atom bomb.

P-61 BLACK WIDOW

NIGHT FIGHTER
SPAN 66'   LENGTH 48' 11"

THE DOC WHO HEARD THE BOYS WERE GOING TO HAVE A "DANCE" SATURDAY NIGHT-

FLIGHT SURGEON

MEDICINAL ALCOHOL 190 PROOF

U.S. APC'S 5 GROSS

SOMETIMES IT JUST *SEEMED* LIKE THIS-

3 APC'S EVERY 2 HRS... MARK FOR DUTY! NEXT!

SICK CALL: 0900-0915 EVERY OTHER TUES.

MOST FLIGHT SURGEONS, GOD BLESS 'EM, FLEW WITH THE TROOPS OCCASIONALLY-

HEY DOC, HOW YOU MAKIN' OUT WITH THAT COMBAT FATIGUE STUDY OF YOURS?

RUPPER

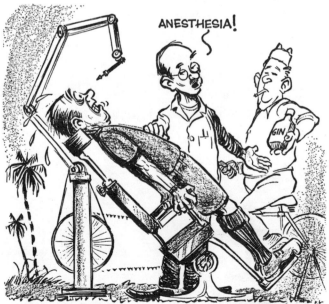

ANESTHESIA!

GIN

EQUIPMENT AND SUPPLIES WERE LIMITED IN SOME AREAS-

FIGHTER PILOTS

Oh there are no fighter pilots down in Hell
Oh there are no fighter pilots down in Hell
The place is full of queers
Navigators, Bombardiers
But there are no fighter pilots down in Hell!

Oh there are no fighter pilots in the States
Oh there are no fighter pilots in the States
They are off to foreign shores
Making mothers out of whores
Oh there are no fighter pilots in the States!

Oh the bomber pilot's life is just a farce
Oh the bomber pilot's life is just a farce
The automatic pilot's on
He's reading novels in the john
Oh the bomber pilot's life is just a farce!

Oh there are no fighter pilots up in Fifth
Oh there are no fighter pilots up in Fifth
The place is full of brass
Sitting 'round on their fat ass
Oh there are no fighter pilots up in Fifth!

Oh it's naughty, naughty, naughty but it's nice
If you ever do it once you'll do it twice
It'll wreck your reputation
But increase the population
Oh it's naughty, naughty, naughty but it's nice!

GRACE

TORPEDO BOMBER

Above, god-like, he pirouettes and whirls
As toward the guns, us fighter-jocks he hurls.
And this we'd like to do as we attack—
Reach out our hands and choke that bloody FAC!

FAC-TO-FIGHTER-JOCKS—

I HAVEN'T SEEN ANY GROUND FIRE — IT'S A GOOD TARGET. C'MON IN!

12,000 FT.

1000 FT.

P.S. GUESS WHO GETS HOSED?

THEN THERE'S THE FAC WHO'S BIG ON TRIG — AT NIGHT, YET!

OKAY, COBRA LEAD, THE MARKERS ARE LYIN' NORTH-EAST TO SOUTHWEST, AND THEY ARE SOUTHEAST OF A ROAD THAT RUNS NORTHWEST TO SOUTHEAST. NOW, 1000 METERS FROM THE S.W. MARKER AND ⅓ THE DISTANCE BETWEEN THE MARKERS TO THE WEST OF THE NORTHEAST MARKER YU....

HEY, LEAD! THEY REALLY SIEVED YOU ON THAT PASS!! NOW PUT YOUR NEXT BOMB 10 FEET TO THE LEFT OF THE LAST ONE!

THE LAST STRAW—

I WANT YOU TO GET THAT GUN SITE THAT JUST CHEWED UP THE F-4 FLIGHT AHEAD OF YOU---

NAPALM ONLY

The legendary Earl B. "Earthquake Magoon" McGovern, a one-time wing man of mine made the landing shown here at Mitchell Air Force Base one winter. After World War II, "Earthquake" became a soldier of fortune in China and "bought the farm" in a C119 at Dien Bien Phu.

"Earthquake" was one of the most interesting characters I ever met. He looked like John L. Lewis with a hangover and had a heart as big as a barn. His sense of humor was rather droll and he broke up more than one control tower with antics like this.

OLD BEER BOTTLE

It was only an old beer bottle
A floatin' o'er the foam
It was only an old beer bottle
A million miles from home
In it was a message
On which these words were written
Whoever finds this bottle
Finds the beer all gone.

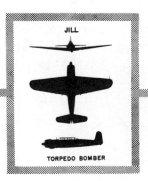

JILL

TORPEDO BOMBER

To tell the world in line-of-sight
That you're a horse's rear,
Just mash the mike before you think,
And everyone will hear.

111

Were any of us really satisfied with things as they were? Of course not! By applying a little effort we could invariably make them worse.

A thunder storm penetration in a bomber with the comfort of a crew and multiengines around you is one thing. But to do it in a skitterish, single engine fighter is something else again. To approximate the reading of an instrument panel during such an event, try bouncing up and down on the couch and reading a newspaper while s o m e o n e turns a thousand watt light off and on rapidly.

As mentioned earlier in this book, the menus -- particularly at overseas stations -- were rather limited. Spam was the main staple. It wasn't until 1950 that I could look a piece of the stuff in the eye again.

B-32 DOMINATOR

HEAVY BOMBER
SPAN 135'   LENGTH 82' 11"

THE MOUSE SONG

(Tune: The Girl I Left Behind Me)

Oh . . . The liquor was spilt on the bar room floor
And . . . The bar was closed for the night
When . . . Out of his hole the little mouse crept
And . . . He sat in the pale moonlight.

He . . . Licked up the liquor on the bar room floor
Then . . . On his haunches he sat
And . . . All night long you could hear him roar:
"Bring on your God damn cat, hic, cat, hic, cat!"

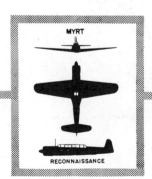

Psychologists, ponder!
And say, if you can:
Did the man make the hat,
Or the hat make the man?

AIRMEN'S HEADGEAR-WWII TYPE

FIRST SGTS AND CAMPAIGN HATS WERE MADE FOR EACH OTHER—

'TACTICAL OFFICERS' (GROUND POUNDERS) LOOKED LIKE THEY HAD A DISCUS IN THE BRIM

GREASE MONKEYS HAD THEIR 'SKIPPY' MODELS

564th

ANYONE KNOW WHY THESE *G! DINKIES WERE CALLED 'OVERSEAS' CAPS?

GANGPLANK

THEN THERE WERE THOSE FLEECE-LINED BEAUTIES THAT ITCHED LIKE HELL.

TROPICS

BUT *NOTHING* COULD MATCH THE '50-MISSION CRUSH'!

HI YA, GIRLS!

115

Back in the days when an airplane without a propeller was treated with suspicion and awe, one Lieutenant "Dusty" Rhoades (all Rhoades in the air force are "Dusty"), a jet fighter instructor at Nellis Air Force Base, created a legend when he made an unscheduled RON at a SAC base.

This sequence needs little explanation except to say that if you've never been on a SAC base when they're pulling a security inspection, you don't know what security is. Trouble was, those SAC types didn't have the same sense of humor "Dusty" had.

THE MAN BEHIND THE ARMOR PLATED DESK

(Tune: Strip Polka)

Early in the morning
When the engines start to roar
You can see the old goat standing
Beside his office door
He'll be sweating out the takeoff
As he's often done before
The man behind the armor plated desk.

Four times he's led us up there
And he always led us back
For he circled o'er the I.P.
As we went in to attack
He said, "I'm hard yet fair, boys,
But allergic to ack ack."
The man behind the armor plated desk.

And when the target's sighted
Who inspires our attack?
Who says, "Hundreds may go in, lads
But a few aren't coming back."
Who says, "We'll disregard the minimum
When you suppress the flak."
The man behind the armor plated desk.

And when the mission's over
And debriefing they should be
You can search the whole field over
But not a pilot you will see
For they'll all be at the "O" club
With a mixed drink in their hand
Singing, "The Man Behind the Armor Plated Desk."

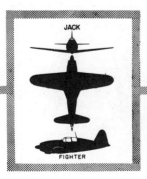

We don't have room for Panel Five.
It shows the colonel, still alive,
Safely clad in a new flak vest—
Base commander at Bluie West . . .

THE BRIEFING -

GENTLEMEN, OUR TARGET FOR TODAY IS.....

RUHRFLACKEN!

IT'S GOING TO BE **ROUGH**, BUT WE'RE *TOUGHER!* WE'RE GOING TO GO RIGHT IN THERE THROUGH THAT FLAK and FIGHTERS AND WE'RE GOING TO LAY THOSE BOMBS RIGHT ON TARGET, AREN'T WE, MEN?!!

RIGHT!

UNFORTUNATELY, I WON'T BE GOING WITH YOU. HQS. HAS ORDERED ME TO REMAIN HERE, *BUT*, MY HEART WILL BE UP THERE WITH YOU ... <u>ALL THE WAY</u>!!

Pilots, especially the air force type, have always been considered a special breed, with their own eccentricities, their own way of doing things and their own brand of stubbornness.

Rolling down the runway with a dedicated (and probably short-lived) hero while one of the fans sputters and clonks can make a co-pilot wish he'd joined the quartermaster corps.

And speaking of stubbornness, there's the old story of General Curtis Le May smoking near his aircraft and being confronted by an eager young guard who admonished the old man that the aircraft might explode. Le May's classic reply: "It wouldn't dare, son."

B-24 LIBERATOR

HEAVY BOMBER
SPAN 110'   LENGTH 67' 2"

TOWER, THIS IS AIR FORCE 2345. I ONLY HAVE **5 GALLONS** OF FUEL LEFT! REQUEST INSTRUCTIONS... *OVER!*

TOWER TO 2345 *!* DON'T PANIC *!!* -- **STAY CALM!** WHAT IS YOUR *EXACT* LOCATION... *OVER!*

CRASH ALARM

AFTER A LONG PAUSE-

I'M PARKED ON THE RAMP. I WAS WONDERING WHERE THE FUEL TRUCK WAS...

PILOT PORTRAITS

THE COPILOT WHO'S JUST SEEN THE PILOT TAKE HIS ST. CHRISTOPHER MEDAL OFF THE INSTRUMENT PANEL & PUT IT IN HIS POCKET...

FAMOUS LAST WORDS

ABORT? **NEGATIVE!** *She'll smooth out!*

ROLL YOUR LEG OVER

If all little girls were like sheep in the pasture
And I was a ram, I would make them run faster.

CHORUS: So roll your leg over, oh roll your leg over
     Oh roll your leg over the man in the moon.

If all little girls were like little white rabbits
And I was a hare, I would teach them bad habits.

If all little girls were like little white flowers
And I was a bee, I would buzz them for hours.

If all little girls were like little white chickens
And I was a rooster, I would give them the dickens.

If all little girls were like little ol' turtles
And I was a turtle, I'd get in their girdles.

The customer is always right . . .
But if his finger's slightly nervous,
And clearly he's equipped to fight,
He may get extra service.

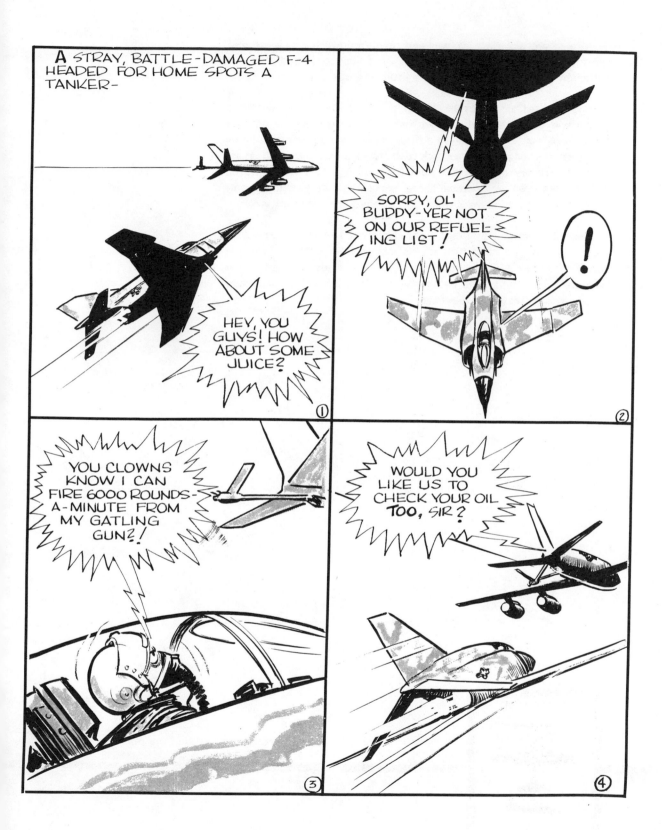

Airmen are a sterling lot, well and rightly known for their intrepid spirit. But on a few rare occasions, for what they considered good and sufficient cause, they may turn just a little bit crooked.

The forward air controller (FAC) shown in the lower, left-hand corner was used effectively in Viet Nam -- the only difference was they were usually airborne, flying in a flivver type observation plane. Some of the stories our pilots came back with after serving a tour with an infantry or artillery outfit in the front lines during WW II and Korea would make even the brashest fighter jock's "There I Was" story pale by comparison. It seems airmen do not have an affinity for tanks.

Regarding weather briefings, I once observed a weather man -- after much figuring and consulting of his instruments -- throw down his pencil and say "Aw, the hell with it." He stuck his head out of the window and observed the weather in the direction of our departure route, saying "Okay, it's clear to go."

INTO THE AIR

Into the air, U. S. Air Force
Into the air, pilots true
Into the air, U. S. Air Force
Keep your nose up in the blue
And when you hear the engines roaring
And the steel props start to whine
Then you can bet the U. S. Air Force
Is on the fighting line!

Ignorance was often bliss
And wisdom sometimes folly,
But angels all worked overtime—
And we won the war, by golly.

In the old timers' air war in Europe, it was noisy, crowded and often very hot. Conditions which, except for the high metal content of the atmosphere, their colleagues on the Aleutian chain would have welcomed.

Why is it that they always pick the lousiest spots on earth to fight a war? The Aleutian chain took the cake for miserable weather. A friend of mine, who returned from this theater of operation, had his feet in water so long that he swore a webbing was starting to grow between his toes.

And if the weather wasn't bad enough, where do you go on a three day pass on an island two miles by four miles?

P-51 MUSTANG

FIGHTER
SPAN 37'   LENGTH 32' 3"

The weather wasn't bad, really-- it was just plain lousy!

and *COLD?* well, you've heard of the brass monkey...

Vegetation was "sparse"...

and you couldn't call your off-duty time exactly "riotous" –

PARTIES, BANQUETS AND BALLS

(Tune: Take Me Out to the Ballgame)

Parties, banquets and balls, boys
Parties, banquets and balls
As President Roosevelt has said before
There's only one way to stay out of a war
That's with parties, banquets and balls, boys
We'll have parties and banquets
And banquets and parties
And balls, balls, balls!

This stereotype, slightly overripe,
May be viewed by some as a lot of tripe.
But though uniforms here are World War II,
Man/mission match still's generically true.

YOU'VE SEEN 'EM IN EVERY CLUB FROM WILLY TO WIESBADEN --- PICK OUT THE (A) FIGHTER JOCK (B) BOMBER PILOT (C) TRANSPORT DRIVER (D) SPECIAL MISSION TYPE (E) BORED BARTENDER (F) GUY WHO GOT THERE EARLY

TOOFER 1 NITE

HOW TO TERRIFY THE FREE-LOADIN' GROUND POUNDERS AT JUST ABOUT LIFTOFF SPEED—

M'GOD WHERE'S THE AIRSPEED?!

AVIATION GLOSSARY

BLIND FLYING HOOD

Wars are won, they say, by the side that makes fewer mistakes. Obviously our valiant air leaders succeeded in forging a sharply-honed, well-oiled, high-geared fighting machine able to rise above the drolleries perpetrated by the chowderheads in our mist. The sequence involving the control tower is probably the oldest saw in aviation,   but no book on this subject would be complete without it.

One of Roger Rudder's wing men is obviously complaining about pulling too many gs -- that physical phenomenum that causes your head to sink just above your belt line while rat racing a fighter.

And just think of the pleasure of jabbing a full colonel with a needle -- in the line of duty.

P-47 THUNDERBOLT

FIGHTER
SPAN 40' 9"   LENGTH 36' 4"

SITUATION: YOU'VE BEEN TRYING TO 'RAISE' THE TOWER FOR OVER 5 MINUTES. OBVIOUSLY YOU'RE 'PUTTING OUT', BUT THE TOWER WON'T ANSWER --- *FINALLY:*

AIR FORCE AIRCRAFT CIRCLING THE FIELD, IF YOU READ THE TOWER — ROCK YOUR WINGS!!

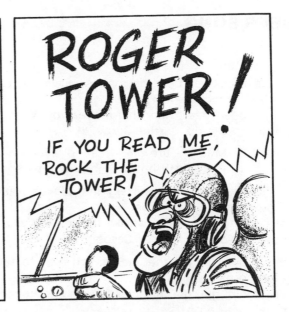

ROGER TOWER!

IF YOU READ ME, ROCK THE TOWER!

COULD I GIVE YOU ANOTHER ONE, COL.? I'M ON O.J.T.

ROGER RUDDER:

OKAY, OKAY! WHO'S THE JOKER COMPLAININ' ABOUT TOO MANY G's?

J. RUDDER, PLEEZE!

OPERAT
460TH
FLT. LDR   RUDDER
            JONES
            SMITH
            JAMES

BEER SONG

For it's beer, beer, beer that makes you want to cheer
In the corps, in the corps
For it's beer, beer, beer that makes you want to cheer
In the Tro-o-o-op Carrier Corps.

CHORUS: My eyes are dim, I cannot see-e-e
        I have (HI) not (HO) brought my specs with me!

For it's whisky, whisky, whisky that makes you feel so frisky
In the corps, in the corps
For it's whisky, whisky, whisky that makes you feel so frisky
In the Tro-o-o-op Carrier Corps.

For it's gin, gin, gin that makes you want to sin
In the corps, in the corps
For it's gin, gin, gin that makes you want to sin
In the Tro-o-o-op Carrier Corps.

For it's vodka, vodka, vodka that makes you feel too hotka
In the corps, in the corps
For it's vodka, vodka, vodka that makes you feel too hotka
In the Tro-o-o-op Carrier Corps.

It's old sauterne, sauterne, sauterne that makes your belly burn
In the corps, in the corps
It's old sauterne, sauterne, sauterne that makes your belly burn
In the Tro-o-o-op Carrier Corps.

It's old vermouth, vermouth, vermouth that makes you feel uncouth
In the corps, in the corps
It's old vermouth, vermouth, vermouth that makes you feel uncouth
In the Tro-o-o-op Carrier Corps.

For it's wine, wine, wine that makes you feel so fine
In the corps, in the corps
For it's wine, wine, wine that makes you feel so fine
In the Tro-o-o-op Carrier Corps.

TEMPEST V

FIGHTER

Perils of instrument night approaches
Differ somewhat for players and coaches,
But for rapid aging, it's hard to beat
A spectator view from a damp right seat . . .

SUSPICIONS CONFIRMED—

IT'S A DARK and STORMY NIGHT; INSIDE THE SNUG GCA SHACK WE SEE—

UH...YER 50 FEET HIGH...NOW YER A HUNNERT FEET HIGH...COMING DOWN...WATCH IT...NOW YER GOING 50 FEET LOW...DECREASE YOUR RATE OF DESCENT...CORRECTING NICELY...OVER THE THRESHOLD...TAKE OVER VISUALLY FOR LANDING...I CALL

AVIATION GLOSSARY

ALTIMETER SETTING

' THE PLACE WHERE THE ALTIMETER SETS— USUALLY HIDDEN BEHIND THE CONTROL COLUMN DURING A TIGHT INSTRUMENT APPROACH '

THE CO-PILOT ON AN INSTRUMENT APPROACH

'CLEARED FOR APPROACH, CEILING 300, VIZ ½...'

'YOU'RE 200 FT. LOW...'

'APPROACHING MINIMUMS, STILL LOW'

'TAKE OVER and LAND VISUALLY'

Nothing much has changed in twenty-five years. Looking back, we seemed little better than boors when we sought to confound with facts those of our brethren who had already made up their minds.

I used to fly co-pilot with an old, crotchety, half-blind geezer who relied more or less on instinct as to when the aircraft needed fuel. I left a trail of sweat across the U.S. on many occasions as the needles bounced around on the zero mark. ("Damn gauges are <u>never</u> accurate!") On one occasion we ran out on one engine and there wasn't enough left in the fuel tanks to dampen a sponge when we landed. The old geezer - who was a high ranking type - is no longer with us.

P-40 WARHAWK

FIGHTER
SPAN 37' 4"   LENGTH 33' 4"

Scene: A USAAF training base: 1942

AIR CORPS 567, MAKE A 360 OVER KELLY BEACON AND LOSE ONE MINUTE IN SPACING, GO AHEAD—

KELLY TOWER

KELLY TOWER, THIS IS 567, FOR YOUR INFORMATION IT TAKES **TWO** MINUTES TO MAKE A 360!

ROGER 567, THEN MAKE A 180 AND **BACK IN!**

Famous last words:

① QUIT SWEATING THOSE *6! FUEL GAUGES!! WE'VE GOT A COUPLE HUNDRED WHEN THEY SHOW "EMPTY."

②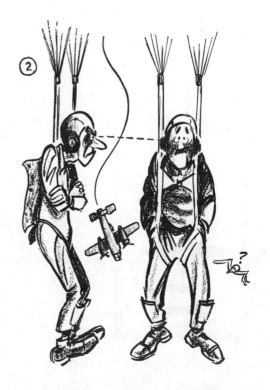

137

DRINK, DRANK, DRUNK

Drunk last night, drunk the night before
Gonna get drunk tonight like I've never been drunk before
For when I'm drunk I'm happy as can be
For I'm a member of the Souse family
Now the Souse family is the best family
That ever came over from old Germany
There's the highland Dutch and the lowland Dutch
The Rotterdam Dutch and the gawdamned Dutch
Singing glorious, glorious
One keg of beer for the four of us
Glory be to God that there are no more of us
For one of us could drink it all alone (damn near!)

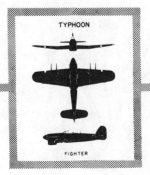

TYPHOON

FIGHTER

See the foe of yesteryear,
The Kamikaze "volunteer."
See the T/O—also changed.
The whole damned world's been rearranged . . .

OUR ADVERSARIES WERE AFFLICTED WITH
THE SAME MENTAL AND PHYSICAL ABERRATIONS
FACED BY G.I.s THE WORLD OVER--

BACK HOME IT WAS BUSINESS AS USUAL-

SOME THINGS _DO_ CHANGE...

Everyone is convinced there is all the time in the world to conduct a war -- then for some strange reason the enemy suddenly begins to take you seriously.

Nothing could instill full discipline in a bunch of ragged irregulars as fast as the imminence of enemy action. The sequence regarding the control tower involves a B24, an airplane with the glide angle of a crowbar. Tower operations seemed somehow to be completely detatched under the most trying circumstances. Sometimes this was a good thing, because when you're up there -- panic stricken with some emergency -- the calm, cool and almost ethereal voice of that guy down there in his snug little haven would bring you back to reality.

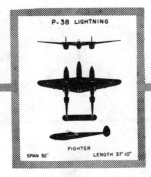

P-38 LIGHTNING

FIGHTER
SPAN 52'   LENGTH 37'10"

REMEMBER THE OLD SAYING, "THERE'S SAFETY IN NUMBERS"?

CONTROL TOWERS SEEMED SO FAR REMOVED FROM THE PROBLEM—

AIR FORCE 801

(Tune: Wabash Cannonball)

Listen to the rumble, and hear old Merlin roar
I'm flying over Moji, like I never flew before
Hear the mighty rush of the slipstream, and hear old Merlin moan
I'll wait a bit and say a prayer and hope it gets me home.

Itazuke tower, this is Air Force 801
I'm turning on the downwind leg, my prop has overrun
My coolant's overheated, the gauge says 1-2-1
You'd better call the crash crew, and get them on the run.

Air Force 801, this is Itazuke tower
I cannot call the crash crew, this is their coffee hour
You're not cleared in the pattern, that is plain to see
So take it on around again, we have some VIP.

Itazuke tower, this is Air Force 801
I'm turning on the downwind leg, I see your biscuit gun
My engine's runnin' ragged, and the coolant's gonna blow
I'm gonna prang a Mustang, so look out down below.

Itazuke tower, this is Air Force 801
I'm turning on the final, and running on one lung
I'm gonna land this Mustang, no matter what you say
I've gotta get my charts fixed up before that Judgment Day.

Air Force 801, this is Judgment Day
You're in Pilot's Heaven, and you are here to stay
You just bought a Mustang, and you bought it well
The famous Air Force 801 was sent straight down to Hell.

Gather round, you Big War jocks,
You guys who flew the Straight,
Or sweated out a Cobra, or left a '38.
Are all these stories true
About the vintage recips
You throttle-benders flew?

HERE ARE A FEW "OLD PILOTS' TALES" THAT'LL STILL START A RHUBARB—

"A P-39 WOULD TUMBLE"

"THE B-26 (MARAUDER) WOULDN'T FLY ON ONE ENGINE"

WOULDN'T YA KNOW! THIS ONLY HAPPENS WHEN THERE'S NO ONE AROUND BUT ME!

HARRY, WE'VE REACHED OUR CRITICAL SINGLE ENGINE ALTITUDE...

"YOU COULDN'T SAFELY BAIL OUT OF A P-38"

"IF THE P-47 HIT 'COMPRESSIBILITY' IN A DIVE THE STICK 'FROZE'"

I WONDER IF A HALF GAINER IS OKAY?

NOTE: ACTUALLY, THE T.O. SAID YOU WERE SUPPOSED TO PULL IT UP IN A 'NEAR STALL', JETTISON THE CANOPY, WALK ACROSS THE STUB WING and DIVE OVER THE BOOM!

A LITTLE THING LIKE THIS COULD RUIN YOUR WHOLE DAY.

15,000 lbs

P.S. THEY ALSO SAID THIS ABOUT THE '38

Here is a fond look back at some of the every day occurrances and annoyances that made life in the service during the Big War such a truly unforgettable experience.

Combat ration booze was slow coming to the Southwest Pacific. And the native stuff would blind a rhino. Our flight surgeons, bless 'em, would stash away a few bottles of "Flip" whisky (Philippine) for just such emergencies. It was blended and aged for the American troops, so you can imagine how long it had been in the keg. It tasted quite a bit like kerosene and water.

The incident involving the landing aircraft (I should say controlled crash of an aircraft) occurred to me the first time members of my family came to witness the neophyte fighter pilot arriving at the home town airport. I believe it was my father-in-law who asked if I always landed that way.

THERE'S A "FIRST" FOR EVERYTHING ~

COMBAT FATIGUE?

NAW, FIRST SHOT OF COMBAT RATION BOOZE!

PUZZLE: PILOT IS OLD 8TH AF HAND BEGINNING HIS 2ND TOUR. CO-PILOT IS BIRD COL -AIR COMMANDER - ON HIS LAST MISSION OF HIS 1ST TOUR. THEIR B-17 HAS LOST 2 FANS ON A MISSION NEAR NEUTRAL SWEDEN. GUESS WHERE THEY WENT...? (ANSWER BELOW)

SIGH!

¡BACK TO BLIGHTY OLD ENGLAND, NATCH!

THE "YA CAN'T WIN" DEPT:

ME, I'M SWEATIN' OUT MY EYES - HAD SO MUCH CARROT JUICE I CAN SEE THROUGH MY EYELIDS! GUESS WHAT I FLUNK? BLOOD PRESSURE!

PROBABLY FROM WORRYIN' ABOUT MY EYES...

FLIGHT SURGEON

EXAMINATIONS

THROW YOUR BUTTS HERE

REMEMBER THE FIRST TIME YOU LANDED WITH SOME MEMBER OF THE FAMILY LOOKING ON...?

WOULDN'T YA KNOW! BEEN GREASIN' 'EM IN FOR A WEEK -- AND NOW...!!

KA-SPRONG!

MY DARLING 39

(Tune: My Darling Clementine)

In the cockpit of the cobra
Trying hard to reach the line
But alas my engine faltered
Fare thee well my 39.

CHORUS: Oh my darling, oh my darling
Oh my darling 39
You are lost and gone forever
Fare thee well my 39.

When you're spinning very flatly
And you've got a worried mind
That's all brother, hit the jumpsack
Bid farewell to your 39.

All the brass hats in our Congress
They have signed the dotted line
They are lucky they just bought it
They don't fly the 39.

MOSQUITO

LIGHT BOMBER-FIGHTER

Turn with a Zero it wouldn't,
Or climb with a sleek One-oh-nine.
But for busting tanks on the tundra
This baby really was fine . . .

THE P-39 (AIRACOBRA) 'THE BIRD NOBODY WANTED'

NOMENCLATURE:

IT'S SO CROWDED IN HERE, I'LL HAVE TO GO OUTSIDE TO CHANGE MY MIND!

PILOT, 1ea., cramped

37mm CANNON (thru prop shaft)

(AUTOMOBILE TYPE DOOR!)

ENGINE, Liquid cooled!

TRICYCLE GEAR (very big in 1939)

THE 'COBRA HAD A PROPENSITY FOR SPINNING *VERY* FLAT... (AND 'TUMBLING').

30 YEARS FROM NOW SOMEBODY 'LL CALL THIS A FRISBEE!

Basically a good design, the '39 was loaded down with 'goodies' at the expense of performance. (Sound familiar?)

> DON'T GIVE ME A P-39
> WITH AN ENGINE THAT'S MOUNTED BEHIND,
> IT WILL TUMBLE AND ROLL
> AND DIG A BIG HOLE —
> DON'T GIVE ME A P-39
> — OLD AAF BALLAD

Spurned by the AAF and RAF, 39's found a warm welcome in the Russian Air Force —

A GAZELLE SHE AIN'T — A RHINO... MAYBE!

EAT AT JOE'S

AIRPORT BOUNDARY

НОБЧY Жepe бут ус apaбc!*

*TRANSLATION: 'MAN! WHAT A CAN OPENER!'

If you can remember Jackie Coogan, you may also recall the Army Air Force's glider fleets that delivered airborne troops in the Burmese jungles as well as behind the Normandy beaches on D-Day. Who's Coogan? Before becoming a U.S.A.A.F. glider pilot, he once played "The Kid" opposite Charlie Chaplin. Now, who's Chaplin?

When the episode of the gliders appeared in my magazine feature, I got a letter from a gentleman who did know Coogan. He wanted to get in touch with a lot of his old former glider pilots . . . most of whom he had not heard from since being discharged in October 1945.

F6F HELLCAT

FIGHTER
SPAN 42' 10"   LENGTH 33' 4"

THOSE 'BAMBOO BOMBERS'- THE GLIDERS- AS SEEN BY:

- THE TOW SHIP CREW

-GLIDER PILOTS THEMSELVES

-THE AIRBORNE TROOPS

-SECOND & THIRD WAVE GLIDER PILOTS

- GERMAN GUNNERS

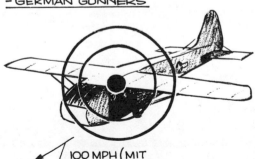

-AND FINALLY, AS SEEN BY THE OCCUPIED COUNTRIES ON D-DAY

I TOOK A LEG

I took a leg from some old table
I took an arm from some old chair
I took the neck from an old beer bottle
And from a broom I took some hair
And then I put them all together
With little bits of string and glue
And I got more lovin'
From that God damn dummy
Than I ever got from you.

The Lightning's design was sure neat,
And its pilots were never effete.
But without jugs in the nose
To keep chill from the toes
All the Lightning jocks suffered cold feet . . .

THE 'LIGHTNING' WAS 'HOT' and COMPLICATED FOR ITS TIME. NEOPHYTE JOCKS WERE USUALLY 'BEHIND IT' THE FIRST 20 HRS OR SO---

YOU STILL THERE, LORD?

THE 4 30's and 20mm CANNON WERE MANUALLY CHARGED FROM THE COCKPIT. BALKY BREECHES CALLED FOR DRASTIC ACTION—

$40,000 FLIGHT TRAINING TO BECOME A *©!m!! CANNON COCKER!

DON'T GIVE ME A P-38,
WITH PROPS THAT COUNTER-ROTATE,
THEY'LL LOOP, ROLL AND SPIN,
BUT THEY'LL SOON AUGER IN,
DON'T GIVE ME A P-38!
—OLD AAF BALLAD

CALLED 'WIDOW-MAKERS' BECAUSE OF A HIGH ACCIDENT RATE, ONE AAF CREWMAN PUT AN ERSATZ DIAL ON THE PANEL THAT SAID IT ALL —

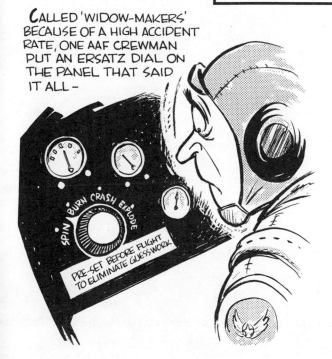

SPIN BURN CRASH EXPLODE

PRE-SET BEFORE FLIGHT TO ELIMINATE GUESSWORK

BUT, REMEMBER, IT WAS THE ONLY AAF WWII FIGHTER THAT COULD COME HOME WITH A PROP FEATHERED!!

Everybody has his problems and foibles in the mad, mad business of pushing yourself through the air from one point to another. But every once in a while you meet somebody of whom it must be said, "There's one in every crowd."

The little radio episode in the P47's took place before the days of inflight refueling -- now the capability exists to transfer fuel from fighter to fighter in a pinch. In those days, we just came back on the sweat of our brow.

Tale two depicts the plague of all air crewmen -- the flight check. Even in the midst of all out conflagration, we were plagued by those busybodies with their checklists who constantly harassed us while in the performance of our appointed duties. Once in a while, we struck back.

F4U CORSAIR

FIGHTER
SPAN 41'   LENGTH 33' 5"

TWO TRUE TALES:

Scene: CBI; A gaggle of "Jugs" (P-47's) on a long, LONG range mission We look at Red 2—

GEEZ, SOLID UNDERCAST, TARGET'S COMIN' UP— FUEL'S LOW, TOO.

RED LEADER THIS IS RED 2 *BINGO*!

*CODE FOR MINIMUM FUEL FOR RETURN TO HOME BASE.

OKAY RED 2 THIS IS RED LEADER, YOU STICK WITH ME— I GOT LOTS!

TALE 2

Scene: A MATS bird way out over the big pond. An overeager check pilot is "giving them hell"

HEH, HEH I'LL FEATHER #3

FEATHERING

FLIGHT ENGINEER

FEATHERING

PUNCH!

FLIGHT ENGINEER

OKAY SIR, IT'S YOUR TURN AGAIN!

CO-PILOT'S LAMENT

(Tune: The Cowboy's Lament)

I'm the co-pilot, I sit on the right
It's up to me to be quick and bright
I never talk back or I'll have regrets
And I must remember what the captain forgets.

I make out the flight plan and study the weather
Pull up the gear and stand by to feather
Make out the mail forms and do the reporting
And fly the old craft when the captain is snoring.

I take the readings and adjust the power
Put on the heaters when we're in a shower
Tell where we are on the darkest night
And do all the book work without any light.

I call for my captain and buy him Cokes
I always laugh at his corny jokes
And once in a while when his landings are rusty
I come through with "Gawd, but it's gusty!"

All in all, I'm a general stooge
As I sit to the right of this overall Scrooge
But maybe some day with great understanding
He'll soften a bit and give me a landing.

—Capt. A. Keith Murray

BARRACUDA

TORPEDO-BOMBER

To sleep, perchance to dream. Aye, there's the rub—
I cannot beat the major with a club!
With all his wrinkles, bags, and rank,
I cannot say, "You and this whole trip stank!"

Well, we did learn how to fly and even to land, but what was sad was that we rarely had a chance to take along as passengers those sadistic creatures who tortured us in the Link Trainers. Their hearts were colder than the metal and glass of the instruments we finally came to understand and sometimes even to believe.

"Needle, ball, airspeed" was the basic flight group -- and keeping an aircraft straight and level on them in the soup was like walking a tightrope with a blindfold on.

Nowadays, pilots fall back on these items when all other instruments fail. But then, the basic equipment has improved, too.

CGA operators lived a lonely life locked in a trailer somewhere down there on the ground and to acknowledge their presence brought out the best in them.

FM WILDCAT

FIGHTER

SPAN 38'   LENGTH 29' 1"

UNDER THE HOOD "NEEDLE, BALL, AIRSPEED" GAVE SOME PECULIAR SENSATIONS—

AHA! STRAIGHT AND LEVEL!

AND IN THE LINK TRAINER, A SADIST ON THE 'ROUGH AIR' CONTROL COULD RUIN YOUR WHOLE DAY--

I *LIKE* INSTRUCTORS LIKE THIS--THEY MAKE ME WANT TO LIVE THROUGH THE WAR!

NOWADAYS, HOWEVER, AUTOMATION & COMPUTERS HAVE TAKEN THE ELEMENT OF ERROR OUT OF INSTRUMENT LANDINGS

693, THIS IS GCA... YOUR POSITION IS DOWNWIND 3 MILES SOUTHEAST...

FW 693

—AND THERE'S ALWAYS ANOTHER SIDE TO A COIN --

GCA

SOME PILOT *THANKED* HIM FOR A GOOD RUN!

LLOYD GEORGE

(Tune: Onward Christian Soldiers)

Lloyd George knows my father
Father knows Lloyd George.
  (Repeat ad nauseum)

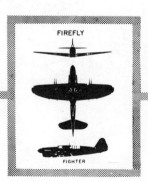

FIREFLY

FIGHTER

New Second Johns thought her a sentence of doom—
Not many runways then had enough room.
But once in the air, with a pair of fans turning,
Brother, this baby just kept on churning . . .

THE MARTIN B-26 'MARAUDER'
'THE FLYING PROSTITUTE'
(IT HAD NO VISIBLE MEANS OF SUPPORT)

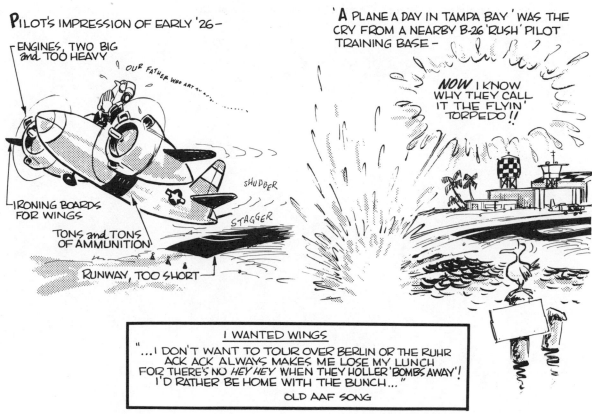

PILOT'S IMPRESSION OF EARLY '26 –

ENGINES, TWO BIG and TOO HEAVY

OUR FATHER WHO ART IN...

IRONING BOARDS FOR WINGS

TONS and TONS OF AMMUNITION

RUNWAY, TOO SHORT

SHUDDER

STAGGER

'A PLANE A DAY IN TAMPA BAY' WAS THE CRY FROM A NEARBY B-26 'RUSH' PILOT TRAINING BASE –

NOW I KNOW WHY THEY CALL IT THE FLYIN' TORPEDO!!

> **I WANTED WINGS**
>
> "...I DON'T WANT TO TOUR OVER BERLIN OR THE RUHR
> ACK ACK ALWAYS MAKES ME LOSE MY LUNCH
> FOR THERE'S NO *HEY HEY* WHEN THEY HOLLER 'BOMBS AWAY'!
> I'D RATHER BE HOME WITH THE BUNCH..."
>
> OLD AAF SONG

FLYING AT MURDEROUSLY MEDIUM ALTITUDES, 26's ATTRACTED FLAK LIKE A MAGNET –

ULP! A GUY COULD GET OUT and WALK ON THAT FLAK!

397TH BOMB GP. MARKINGS

Flak Bait

HELL, YES, WE GOT PROBLEMS! SEND US MORE OF THE DAMNED AIRPLANES!

BOMB TONNAGE

ACCIDENTS

MAINT.

C.O. 22ND BOMB GP.

NOTE: DESPITE EARLY PROBLEMS THE 'MYSTICAL MARAUDER' TURNED IN AN UNPARALLED COMBAT RECORD!

159

Beauty, they say, is in the eye of the beholder. That plane you flew may have been only a bucket of bolts, but the mental pictures it evoked in those beholden to it could really turn out to be beauts.

This plate doesn't need words -- particularly if you happen to "serve" in one of these categories.

PV-I VENTURA

MEDIUM BOMBER
SPAN 65' 6"   LENGTH 51' 9"

That magnificent WW II flying machine of yours — as seen by:

The manufacturer—

Your crew Chief—

The Flying Safety Officer—

Supply—

Armament—

Communications—

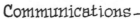

Your wife—

...and you—

A MAN WITHOUT A WOMAN

A man without a woman
Is like a ship without a sail
Is like a boat without a rudder
Like a kite without a tail.

A man without a woman
Is like a shipwreck on the sand
But if there's one thing worse in the universe
It's a woman, I said a woman
I mean a woman without a man.

For you can roll a silver dollar
'Cross the bar room floor
And it will roll because it's round
And a woman never knows what a good man she's got
Until she turns him down.

So honey listen, now honey listen to me
I want you to understand
That a silver dollar goes from hand to hand
While a woman goes from man to man.

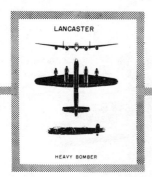

LANCASTER

HEAVY BOMBER

Pop, Pop, Sputter, Bang!
Is the Maytag going to prang?
Sputter, Sputter, Bang, Bump!
I thought the pilot said to jump!

BRIEFING FOR OUR FIRST NIGHT
DUAL RIDE - PRIMARY FLYING
SCHOOL, DOS PALOS, CALIF. (1942)

AND SO IT CAME TO PASS THAT
THEY LEAPED OFF IN THEIR
'MAYTAG MESSERSCHMITTS' (PT-22's)

OUR INSTRUCTOR IS OVERCOME
WITH THE BEAUTY OF THE NIGHT...
DUMBJOHN CAN'T HEAR SO THE BOSS
THROTTLES BACK, AND...

YEP, YOU GUESSED IT—

It's never been much of a treat to bail out of an airplane, but I have to admit that there's been considerable progress in the art of retrieval since the days when a raft was where you stood a good chance of spending the rest of the war.

Pilots over Vietnam probably carried more survival gear than we did in WW deuce. In those days before miniaturization, the stuff was just heavier and bulkier. Yet, even with all the communications and co-ordination that exist today, there is ever-present that human factor -- or Murphy's Law ("If anybody can foul it -- Murphy can.")

WWII FIGHTER PILOT SURVIVAL GEAR
(S.W. PACIFIC)

I'LL GO RIGHT THROUGH MY CHUTE HARNESS WITH ALL THIS CRUD ON...

MAE WEST
WHISTLE
SHARK REPELLANT
LIGHT
"POOPY" SUIT
RATIONS

45 CAL PISTOL
JUNGLE KIT
DINGHY
CHUTE
MAPS
KNIFE

IF YOU SURVIVED THE CHUTE OPENING SHOCK, A CONVERTED B17 ('DUMBO') MIGHT DROP A WHOLE LIFE BOAT ON YOU--

VIETNAM TECHNOLOGY MADE RESCUE ALMOST ROUTINE --- *ALMOST*

PUNCH OUT, OL' BUDDY! WE'VE STOPPED A *6 ~!6 SAM!

HOO BOY! 'HANOI HILTON' HERE WE COME!

MAYDAY! MAYDAY! THIS IS TIGER LEAD--

ROGER, TIGER LEAD. THIS IS RESCUE SHIP. GIVE ME YOUR TYPE ACFT, HEADING, ALTITUDE & AIRSPEED--

SAVE A FIGHTER PILOT'S LIFE

(Tune: Throw a Nickel on the Drum)

Oh, I lined up with the runway and headed for the ditch
I looked down at my prop, my God, it's in high pitch
I pulled back on the stick and rose into the air
Glory, Glory, Hallelujah, how did I get there?

CHORUS: Oh Hallelujah, Oh Hallelujah
          Throw a nickel on the grass
          Save a fighter pilot's ass
          Oh Hallelujah, Oh Hallelujah
          Throw a nickel on the grass
          And you'll be saved!

I started in to buzz, I thought that I was clear
And when I clipped the flagpole, I knew the end was near
I met the flying board, and they gave me the works
Glory, Glory, Hallelujah, what a bunch of jerks!

Fouled up my crosswind landing, my left wing touched the ground
Got a call from Mobile, "Pull up and go around!"
I racked that (name of a/c) in the air a dozen feet or more
The bastard snapped, I'm on my back, oh save me (name of Sq. CO)!

Oh, I flew the traffic pattern, to me it looked alright
And when I made my final turn, my God, I racked it tight
The engine coughed and sputtered, the ship began to weave
Mayday, Mayday, Col. (Wing CO), Spin instructions please!

Strafin' on the panel, I made my pass too low
Came a call from tower, "One more and home you go!"
I pulled that (name of a/c) in the blue, she hit a high-speed stall
Now I won't see my mother when the work's all done this fall!

Previously, we touched on how to bail out of a P-38. This brought forth a pilot's manual which contained—honest Injun—the quotes on the opposite page.

ON BAILING OUT-

"ONCE YOU HAVE STARTED FALLING YOUR FIRST INCLINATION MAY BE TO SEE HOW FAST YOU CAN GET THAT CHUTE OPEN. IF THIS IS YOUR INCLINATION- *CONTROL IT!*"

"THE IMPORTANT THING TO REMEMBER IS: DO NOT RISK DAMAGING YOUR CHUTE BY OPENING IT AT HIGH SPEEDS"

"SOME PILOTS STILL BELIEVE THAT OLD FABLE ABOUT COUNTING THREE WHEN PULLING. FOR OUR MONEY THAT IS JUST ANOTHER RUMOR"

"WHENEVER POSSIBLE WAIT UNTIL YOU GET THAT 'OLD FLOATING FEELING'"

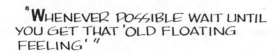

It used to be a pretty easy business to get off the ground. But those days are gone forever. Now, with planes big enough to carry Barnum & Bailey's whole circus and with all that air traffic, you might just as well be driving the old Chevy and fighting the freeways.

It is an actual fact in today's Air Force that the preflight for a large bomber or cargo aircraft might actually start the day before you're scheduled to take off -- and, brother, that's some pre-takeoff checklist.

The guys who transmit clearances to you from the tower or departure control still speak in Sanskrit and deliver at somewhere around 200 words per minute. Some day, I suppose, this too will be automated.

"Getting Off the Ground is Half the Fun"---
PREFLIGHT, CIRCA 1944

and there's always those sadists on the radio--

BLESS 'EM ALL (WW II)

A crippled old Fortress was leaving the Ruhr
Bound for old Blimy's shore
Blood all over the floor
Many a Focke Wulf filled her with lead
Many a Messerschmitt, too
Shot off her bollix, shot up her hydraulics
So cheer up my lads, bless 'em all.

CHORUS: Bless 'em all, bless 'em all
         The long, the short and the tall
         Bless all the corporals and their bastard sons
         For we're saying farewell to them all
         As back to their billets they crawl
         There'll be no promotions this side of the ocean
         So cheer up my lads, bless 'em all.

WARWICK

AIR SEA RESCUE
MEDIUM BOMBER

Forgive the IPs lots of tricks
From which these monsters get their kicks,
But here's a ploy that's just too shoddy,
So, Sarge, let's jettison the body . . .

As we've noted on the preceding pages several times before, nothing -- well, hardly anything -- seemed to work out in the crisp and correct manner outlined in the book. It made you wonder if maybe you'd have been better off in the infantry.

There is nothing quite so humiliating as preparing everyone for starting the right engine and then inadvertently cranking the left. It's hard on ground crewmen, too.

A gossport was a speaking tube between the instructor and student pilot. Holding the speaking end into the airstream could cause quite a draft between the student pilot's ears. Nowadays instructors scream into the intercom at 120 decibels. The effect is the same.

PV-2 HARPOON

MEDIUM BOMBER
SPAN 75'   LENGTH 52

CLEAR RIGHT!

ENGAGE

POP! BANG!
RRRRRR?

P.S. IT'S HAPPENED TO MANY A GOOD MAN—

REMEMBER THE GOOD OLD TRAINING DAYS WHEN THE INSTRUCTOR HELD THE FUNNEL END OF THE GOSPORT OUT IN THE SLIPSTREAM TO GET YOUR ATTENTION?

FUN, EH?

IF YOU DON'T THINK WE WERE A 'MIXED BAG', OBSERVE THIS U.S. PILOT, BASED IN ITALY, FLYING AN ENGLISH 'MOSQUITO' ABOUT TO BUZZ OFF ON TDY FROM FRANCE TO BRITAIN—

O/S STRIPES—
(LOOK LIKE
RANK OF
FRENCH CAPT.)

RAF
WINGS

U.S.
WINGS

'IKE'
JACKET

PINKS

RAF
BOOTS

173

BLESS 'EM ALL (Korea)

Bless 'em all, bless 'em all
The long and the short and the tall
Bless old man Lockheed for building this jet
But I know a guy who is cursing him yet
For he tried to go over the wall
With his tiptanks, his tailpipes and all
The needles did cross and the wings did come off
Cheer up my lads, bless 'em all.

Well, bless 'em all, bless 'em all
The needle, the airspeed and ball
Bless all those instructors who taught me to fly
Sent me to solo and left me to die
If ever your blow jet should stall
Well, you're due for one hell of a fall
No lilies or violets for dead fighter pilots
Cheer up my lads, bless 'em all.

Bless 'em all, bless 'em all
The long and the short and the tall
Bless all the sergeants and their bloody sons
Bless all the corporals, the fat-headed ones
I'm saying goodbye to them all
The long and the short and the tall
Here's to you and lots others you can shove it up brothers
I'm going back home in the fall.

We've sometimes wondered if the armament chief
Lives on a diet of uncooked beef.
Here we learn that his temper—seldom stable—
Has been fragged by the ops guys, not by the table!

THE ARMAMENT CHIEF

The invasion of "Fortress Europe" by the greatest armada of aircraft ever assembled was launched on D-Day, June 6, 1944. Gliders, transports, bombers and fighters all rode shotgun for the great movement across the Channel. All in all, it was quite a show.

The air traffic routes across the Channel looked like the Los Angeles freeway. If you missed your spot in the lineup, you had to stay where you were -- there wasn't room anywhere else. Anything that didn't have big black and white stripes painted on it was to be shot down. Fortunately, the Germans had not heard about our "invasion" markings.

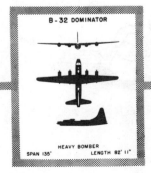

B - 32 DOMINATOR

HEAVY BOMBER
SPAN 135'   LENGTH 82' 11"

JUNE 6, 1944

ON THAT FATEFUL DAY, ALL AIR-
CRAFT WERE MARKED WITH BIG,
BROAD BLACK & WHITE "INVASION"
STRIPES -"RECOGNITION", THEY SAID.

AND WHY THE HELL NOT? I MIGHT HAVE TO BAIL OUT, Y'KNOW!

NO STEP

AND THOSE PHOTO RECCE
PILOTS! ARMED WITH ONLY A .45
CAL. PISTOL,THEY FLEW SOME OF
THE HAIRIEST MISSIONS OF ALL...

NOW I KNOW WHY THESE ARE CALLED "DICING" MISSIONS! IT'S SNAKE EYES ALL THE WAY!

CLICK
CLICK
CLICK
CLICK
CLICK

GLIDERS-LITTLE ADVANCED FROM
THE WRIGHT BROS. DESIGN-CARRIED
THOUSANDS OF TROOPS BEHIND THE
ENEMY LINES...

IT'S NOT THE RIDE OVER THAT GETS ME - IT'S THE LONG WALK BACK! I'M A PILOT!

IT WAS A LONG, LONG DAY
IN JUNE AND MANY A DEBRIEF-
ING OFFICER THAT NIGHT GOT
A MONOSYLLABIC ANSWER-

Z

-AND MAY I QUOTE YOU ON THAT?

WRECK OF THE OLD '97

There were 97 airplanes warming up on the apron
Not enough room you could see
Now the first ninety-six were of recent construction
But the last one was a Fifty-one D.

She was old 97 and she had a fine record
But she hadn't been flown that year
And she creaked and groaned when they started her engine
For she knew that her time was near.

A Second Lieutenant wandered into Operations
And he asked for a ship or two
And they said, "Young man, we are very short of airplanes
But we'll see what we can do.

"Now the first forty-seven are reserved for Majors
And the Captains have the next forty-nine
But there's one more ship on the end of the apron
The last ship upon the line."

He was headed for Nadzab and from there to Guzab
And he had to make that flight
So he said, "O.K., if you'll give me a clearance
I will get there sometime tonight."

He flew through rain and he flew through a snowstorm
Till the light began to fail
When he found a railroad going his direction
And he said, "I'll get there by rail."

He flew down a valley and he dodged through the mountains
And he kept that road in sight
Till the rails disappeared through a tunnel in the mountains
And he ended his last, long flight.

There was old 97 with her nose in the mountain
And her wheels upon the track
And her throttle was bent in the forward position
But her engine was facing back.

Now ladies please listen and heed my warning
From this time ever on
Never speak harsh words to your flyboy husband
He may leave you and never return.

Here, barracks wisdom we distill—
If things can go amiss, they will . . .
A foe misjudged will get the kill . . .
Rank had its dues, and has 'em still . . .
And you, my son, need never fear
If you neglect to volunteer!

It has been more than twenty years since America's first big pilot conversion program turned Mustang and Corsair jocks into two- and four-engined drivers who assisted their bretheren in flying the big, fat, slow birds on the tightropes to Berlin. They did a lasting job. Berlin today may still have problems, but two-thirds of the city remains free, thanks to this dedicated band.

JUNE 26, 1948, 'CALLUP DAY' CAUGHT MANY CREWS IN VARIOUS STATES OF READINESS —

WELL SIR, Y'SEE WE WERE ON THE 3RD TEE AT HICKAM AND...

RHEIN MAIN

THE WEATHER? LET'S HEAR HOW IT WAS IN GERMANY FROM AN OLD EXPERT —

IT WAS LOUSY, JUST PLAIN LOUSY!

THE GROUND CREWS, BLESS 'EM, WORKED AROUND THE CLOCK. THOSE UNLOADING CARGOS LOOKED LIKE THIS —

HAULING COAL HAD ITS LIGHTER SIDE —

YOU GIVE ME THAT 'COAL DUST TWINS' ONE MORE TIME...AN' POW!

LE MAY'S COAL & FEED CO.

HEY FELLAS! I'M A WALKIN' CASSEROLE!

CEREAL   MACARONI

FLOUR   BEANS   POTATOES

SOMETHING *HAD* TO BREAK THE MONOTONY – AND, AS USUAL, IT WAS GI-INSPIRED SONGS AND DITTIES

TEN TONS TO TEMPELHOF

FULDA RADIO, THIS IS 'SMALL CHANGE ON THE RANGE'

OR (YUK, YUK) 4 NICKELS OVER FULDA

BIG WILLIE, HERE'S OL' 77 WITH "A LOAD OF COAL FOR OUR DAILY GOAL"

TALK ABOUT FAST TURN-AROUND TIMES! GANDER AT THE BRIEFING TEAM AT WORK IN A C-54 AT 'BIG B'

HERE'S YOUR WEATHER-READY TO COPY?

ROGER

LATRINE PILOTS ONLY

AND THERE WERE THOSE BIERSTUBE LOTHARIOS –

I CONCERN MYSELF WITH FLOUR & POTATOES – ALTHOUGH I'M NOT ABOVE HAULING MACARONI

WEARY? MAN, THOSE EARLY DAYS WERE *TOUGH* ON A GUY!

LE'SEE, 4 BAGS – I MUST'VE BEEN HERE 4 WEEKS NOW.

FLY SAFE

IT ALL SEEMED WORTH IT WHEN SOME SCRAWNY GERMAN KID OFFER-ED HIS OR HER MOST PRIZED POSSESS-ION TO YOU IN GRATITUDE ~

MARY ANN McCARTHY

(Tune: Battle Hymn of the Republic)

Mary Ann McCarthy she went out to dig some clams
Mary Ann McCarthy she went out to dig some clams
Mary Ann McCarthy she went out to dig some clams
But she never got a Goddam sonofa-bitchofa-clam!!

CHORUS: All that Mary got was oysters
         All that Mary got was oysters
         All that Mary got was oysters
         But she never got a Goddam sonofa-bitchofa-clam!

She dug up all the mud there was in San Francisco bay
She dug up all the mud there was in San Francisco bay
She dug up all the mud there was in San Francisco bay
But she never got a Goddam sonofa-bitchofa-clam!

HALIFAX

HEAVY BOMBER

Although your record's quite impressive,
Your arrogance now seems excessive.
When tallying this morning's score,
One's as good as sixty-four!

LET'S HAVE A PARTY!

Parties make the world go 'round
World go 'round, world go 'round
Parties make the world go 'round
Let's have a party!

SOLO	CHORUS
Now, we're gonna tear down the bar in the officers' club	BOO!
We're gonna build us a new bar!	RAY!
It's only gonna be one foot wide	BOO!
But it's gonna be a mile long!	RAY!
There's gonna be no bartenders at our bar	BOO!
There's only gonna be barmaids!	RAY!
Our barmaids will wear long dresses	BOO!
Made out of cellophane!	RAY!
You can't take our barmaids to your bunks	BOO!
They take you to their bunks!	RAY!
You can't sleep with our barmaids	BOO!
They don't let you sleep!	RAY!
Soda's gonna be ten bucks a glass	BOO!
Whiskey's free!	RAY!
Only one to each pilot	BOO!
Served in buckets!	RAY!
We're gonna throw all the beer in the river	BOO!
And then we'll all go swimming!	RAY!
Now no girls are allowed in the USO hall	BOO!
With their clothes on!	RAY!
There'll be no lovin' on the dance floor	BOO!
And no dancing on the lovin' floor!	RAY!

Parties make the world go 'round
World go 'round, world go 'round
Parties make the world go 'round
Let's have a party!

YORK

CARGO-TRANSPORT

When the work's all done at evening,
When they've beat the Zeke's attacks,
And the morrow is a stand-down,
Then the fighter jocks relax.

And if, around the squadron bar,
Some overly unbend,
They'll leave that last long runway—
Fighter pilots to the end.

HELLO!

We're never too busy to say hello
We're never too busy to say hello
We're never too busy to say hello
HELLO—HELLO—HELLO!

SUNDERLAND

FLYING BOAT

A bold, free spirit charging fierce
Across the fallow land
And don't you like these nice white flowers
I'm holding in my hand?

—Gill Robb Wilson

THE B-36

(Tune: Battle Hymn of the Republic)

The B-36 it flies at 40,000 feet
The B-36 it flies at 40,000 feet
The B-36 it flies at 40,000 feet
But it only drops a teensey, weensey bomb,
Tons and tons of ammunition
Tons and tons of ammunition
Tons and tons of ammunition
But it only drops a teensey, weensey bomb.

A-26 INVADER

MEDIUM BOMBER

*These are excerpts of "orders"
given to Confederate Air Force
crews for a flight from Rebel Field,
Harlingen, Texas to Wright-Pat. Our
thanks to "Col. Throckmorton T.
Beauregard, CAF" for this
aviation classic.*

"Any aircraft with operational compass may serve as flight leader. (Charts published prior to 1936 are not considered reliable and should not be used.) . . . Compass heading 10° to 60° mag. approx. Your route will take you over six states; Okla. is the green one; Missouri is brown; Ill. is yellow; Ind. is red, and Ohio is the tan one on your Texaco map. Care must be used at intersection of US 66 and US 40 east of St. Louis--stay on US 40."

<u>Preflight</u>--
"Next, check stick and throttle positions. If the stick is in your left hand and the throttle is in your right hand, you are in the cockpit backwards. Don't panic! Smile at the crew chief, wave to bystanders and slowly rotate your body 180°."

"When signal is given to taxi, advance the throttle smoothly, hit the 'highblower' switch and jump smoothly over the chocks. Retard the throttle to military power and try to avoid further use of highblower while taxiing as this irritates ground personnel."

"After leaving the ground, pull the nose up smartly, close your eyes and count 10. If contact with the ground has not occurred by that time, continue the mission as briefed. (Note: You may open your eyes for the remainder of the flight if you wish--however, this is optional.)"

189

LAMENT OF THE RESERVIST

(Tune: "Cigareets" and Whisky)

I was a civilian and flew on weekends
No sweat about clanks and no sign of the bends
But I am a retread and older I grow
Now I fly a Mustang, it's old and it's slow.

CHORUS: Sinuiju and Anak, Sinanju and Sinmak
          They'll drive you crazy, they'll drive you insane.
          Quad fifties and forties and one hundred sorties
          They'll drive you crazy, they'll drive you insane!

Oh, once I was happy and I flew a jet
At 35,000 how fat can you get?
They sent me to Nellis for six weeks to train
They gave me a Mustang, it's no aero-plane!

We strafed and we bombed and we shot air to air
Then off to Korea, we're fouled up for fair
We came to K-Four-Six to fly with this Group
My hair's turning gray and my wings have a droop!

I flew my first mission and it was a snap
Just follow the leader, don't look at a map
But now I've got eighty and lead a sad flight
Go out on armed recce and can't sleep at night!

Went up to Mig Alley, S-2 said no sweat
If I had not looked 'round, I'd be up there yet
Six Migs jumped our ass and the leader yelled "Break!"
Sixty-one and three thousand, how my knees did shake!

If I live through a hundred and they ask for more
I'll tell them to shove it, my ass is too sore
They can ram it and jam it for all that I care
Just give me a Wing job, a desk and a chair!

B-25 MITCHELL

MEDIUM BOMBER

Rest and Recreation was its official name
Now the title's changed—tho' the purpose
  is the same.
To the men it's R and R—those letters
  stand for fun.
But to the friendly natives, it means
  "Romp and Run".

REMEMBER HOW IT WAS *GOING* ON R and R?...

AND COMING BACK?

EINSTEIN WAS RIGHT— TIME *and* DISTANCE CAN CHANGE MATTER.

WHAT SHE *REALLY* LOOKED LIKE

LORRY STOP

IN THE PACIFIC THEATER IT WAS HARD TO TELL WHEN A GUY HAD BEEN ON R and R—

BEFORE

AFTER

THE "ASIATIC" STARE (LOOK- ING 20 YDS IN A 20 FT. ROOM.

THE "WHAT-THE- HELL-AM-I-DOING BACK-HERE-I- COULD-GET- KILLED" LOOK.

KOREA

(Tune: I'm Looking Over a Four-Leaf Clover)

I'm looking over a well fought over
Korea that I abhor
One for the money
And two for the show
Ridgeway said stay
But we want to go.
There's no use explaining
Why we're remaining
We've got what we're fighting for
Korea, Korea—and diarrhea
To make the rice grow some more.

P-51 MUSTANG

FIGHTER

Missing an easy enemy kill
May be cause for colossal chagrin.
But nothing at all like a critical call
When a fighter jock's all buckled in.

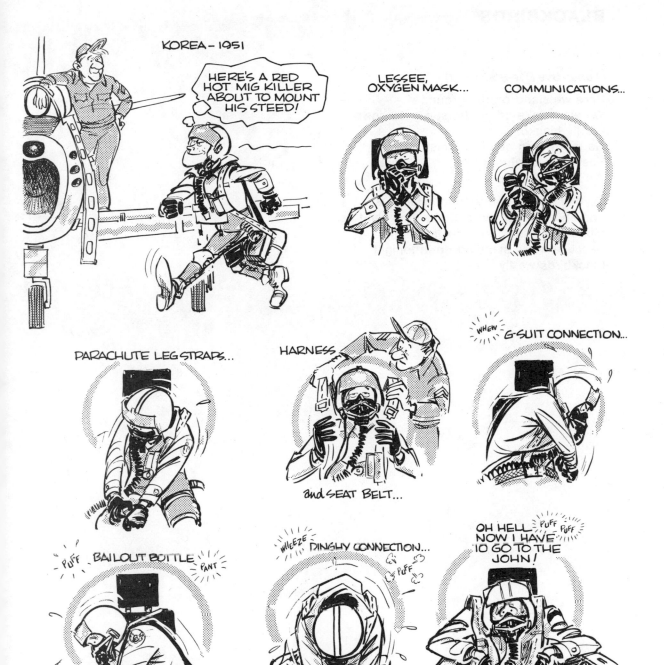

BLACKBIRDS

(Tune: Bye Bye Blackbird)

Here we stand on the ground
We won't take off till the sun goes down
We fly blackbirds . . .
Go in low and come out fast
Keep those fighters off our . . . necks
We fly blackbirds.

No one here can ever understand us
You should hear the malarky they hand us
Mix those drinks and mix 'em right
Because we're standing down tonight
Blackbirds we fly.

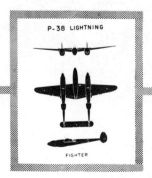

Glory! No more regulations . . .
Rip them down in all the stations!
Ground the guy that tries to make one!
AND LET US ALL FLY LIKE HELL!
—Old AAF Song

AT A FORWARD FIRE BASE DURING THE MOST RECENT UNPLEASANTNESS—

Then there was the newly-minted 2ND LT.—NAVIGATOR TYPE—WHO SHOWED UP AT BASE OPERATIONS FULLY OUTFITTED FOR A SCHEDULED FLIGHT—

*INSPECT and REPAIR AS NECESSARY

And in cadets, you could always scare hell out of yourself and the instructor by switching to an empty tank in the pattern pulling the **GUMP** check—

GAS
UNDERCARRIAGE
MIXTURE
PROP

"G" SUITS AND PARACHUTES

(Tune: Bell Bottom Trousers)

Once there was a barmaid down in Brewery Lane
Her master was so kind to her, her mistress was the same
Along came a pilot, handsome as he could be
He was the cause of all her misery!

CHORUS: Singing "G" Suits and parachutes
          And uniforms of blue
          He'll fly a fighter
          Like his daddy used to do!

Now in the morning before the break of day
A five-pound note he handed her, and this to her did say:
"Take this my darling, for all the harm I've done
For you may have a daughter, and you may have a son
If you have a daughter, put ribbons in her hair
And if you have a son, get the bastard in the air!"

Now the moral of my story as you can plainly see
Is never trust a pilot an inch above your knee
The barmaid trusted one and he went off to fly
Leaving her a daughter to help the time go by!

FINAL CHORUS: Singing "G" Suits and parachutes
                And uniforms of blue
                She'll never fly a fighter
                Like her daddy used to do!

P-47 THUNDERBOLT

FIGHTER

Both of these stories are true, my friend,
And Merced Field was the place.
We yearn to be a dumbjohn again—
Our motto? "Each man an Ace!"

Then there was "der Instruktor" (a cadet) who entertained Class 43E–via radio:

(P.S. THE BRASS NEVER CAUGHT 'IM)

HAIL TO THE SQUADRON

Hail to the Squadron, Hail to the Corps
Hail to all airmen who braved the skies before
We're on the road to victory, thumbs up forever more
Hail to the squadrons flying high
Hail to the men who rule the sky
Hail to the Army, the Army Air Corps.

Early in WW II there was a lot of hysteria and misinformation about Japanese aircraft and pilots. Since the rather fragile Zero could outclimb the P-40 and Japanese pilots rarely attacked unless the advantage was clearly theirs (not a bad idea), PR types had a field day.

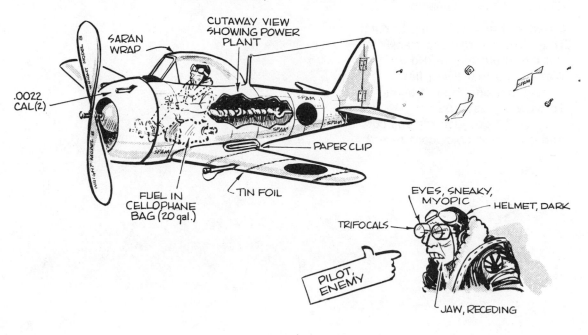

ZERO (THEIRS)

CUTAWAY VIEW SHOWING POWER PLANT

SARAN WRAP

WRIGHT MODEL B

.0022 CAL (2)

PAPER CLIP

TIN FOIL

FUEL IN CELLOPHANE BAG (20 gal.)

EYES, SNEAKY, MYOPIC

HELMET, DARK

TRIFOCALS

PILOT, ENEMY

JAW, RECEDING

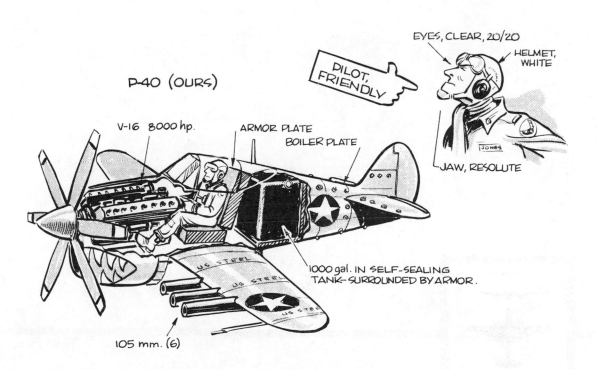

EYES, CLEAR, 20/20

HELMET, WHITE

PILOT, FRIENDLY

P-40 (OURS)

V-16 8000 hp.

ARMOR PLATE

BOILER PLATE

JAW, RESOLUTE

JONES

US STEEL

1000 gal. IN SELF-SEALING TANK-SURROUNDED BY ARMOR.

105 mm. (6)

RAIL CUTTERS

(Tune: Cold, Cold Heart)

I tried so hard, Wild Bill, to cut
That streak of railroad track
But I'm afraid that all I did
Was dodge that flying flak.
I know that one is all it takes
To blow my ass apart
Why can't I get just one rail cut
And melt your cold, cold heart?

A-20 HAVOC

MEDIUM BOMBER

We've had fuel shortages before. For awhile in WWII there wasn't enough 100/130 to fill a Zippo. Higher HQ—in its infinite wisdom— substituted 91 octane for 100/130 in the States. Dubbed "Operation Prang" by pilots, it scattered men and machines from Bangor to Baja.

YOU CAN TELL A FIGHTER PILOT

(Tune: Battle Hymn of the Republic)

By the ring around his eyeball
You can tell a bombardier
You can tell a bomber pilot
By the spread around his rear
You can tell a navigator
By his sextants, maps and such
You can tell a fighter jockey
BUT YOU CAN'T TELL HIM MUCH!

The song above says it all.
Short, fat, lean or tall,
A fighter jock's got lots of class—
Even spread flat on his brass.

① **TWO "SMOULDERING BOULDERS"– FIGHTER JOCKS FRESH FROM OVERSEAS–CHECK INTO THEIR FIRST ZI DUTY STATION.**

HEY, DADDY-O, ASSIGN US ONE OF THEM BUCKETS O' BOLTS OUT THERE! GOT TO GET OUR 4 HOURS!

② **THE B-25 PREFLIGHT WAS A SNAP.**

HELL! 'TAIN'T NOTHIN' BUT TWO FIGHTERS TIED TOGETHER!

RIGHT, ROCK!

HAIL MARY...

FLIGHT ENGINEER

③ **ON TAKEOFF, THINGS SUDDENLY GOT A BIT STICKY–**

WHAT THE..?

..FULL OF GRACE....

POW

SPUT

BAM

KEERASH

④ **LATER:**

WHAD'YA MEAN WHAT HAPPENED?! *MY* ENGINE WAS RUNNIN' ROUGH SO I ABORTED!!

This classic airman's story had its origin in the Panama Canal Zone during WWII where a bunch of bored P-39 and P-40 jocks stood "submarine alert" . . .

TBM AVENGER

TORPEDO-BOMBER
SPAN 54' 2"   LENGTH 40' 9"

EVERY DAY WAS THE SAME. TAXI OUT and SIT IN THE BLAZING SUN FOR 4 HRS ON RUNWAY ALERT.

BOY! NOW THERE'S SOMEBODY THAT'S GOT IT MADE! JUST HANG AROUND IN THE SHADE ALL DAY!

P 40 N-25
S.N. 42 9275
2ND LT. DUMBJOHN PILOT
CREW CHIEF SGT.

!DEA!

THE NEXT DAY A BUNCH OF BANANAS COAXED THE SIMIAN TO THE AIRCRAFT—

NICE BOY! WANNA SIT IN THE NICE AIRPLANE?

AFTER MANY, MANY BUNCHES OF BANANAS, THE APE WOULD EVEN WEAR HELMET, GOGGLES and A CHUTE!

HEH, HEH. NOW BACK TO THE B.O.Q. and SOME GOOD OL' SACK TIME!

THEN ONE DAY THE SIREN WAILED "SCRAMBLE"! THE 2ND JOHN GOT TO THE B.O.Q. WINDOW JUST IN TIME TO SEE HIS FLIGHT TAKE OFF—— ALL OF 'EM!

AND YA WANNA KNOW SOMETHIN'? TODAY, THAT S.O.B. IS MY GROUP COMMANDER!

ODE TO THE B-29

(Tune: Whiffenpoof Song)

We are four little fans who have lost our way, GROWR, GROWR, GROWR
We are four little fans who have gone astray, GROWR, GROWR, GROWR
One third pilot out on the left, one third pilot out on the right
"George" is flying with all his might! GROWR, GROWR, GROWR.

*Many will remember "Operation Crossroads"—
the atom bomb tests at Bikini's blue atoll.
The public recalls the awesome mushroom
clouds. Members of the 58th Wing will never
forget the human drama that unfolded.*

1946 – TASK FORCE 1.52 IS EN ROUTE TO BIKINI FOR THE A-BOMB TESTS....AH, BIKINI !

– THEN THEY LANDED !

NO LOVE ATOLL

POOF!

THE MAIN TOPIC AT THE CLUB BARS WAS –

WHAT *the* THE 💣 BOMB LOOKS LIKE

KWAJALEIN DRESS: PITH HELMET, SHORTS and BOONDOCKERS (PONCHOS WERE ALSO FASHIONABLE!)

ABLE DAY 1 JULY 1946 – WHILE THOUSANDS WATCHED 'DAVE'S DREAM' – A B-29 – DROPPED THE BOMB ON A CAPTIVE TARGET FLEET –

I'M SO NERVOUS.... WHAT IF I MISS ? *

WHRRRRR CHICK CHICK CLICK CLICK WHRRRRR

* HE DID! – BUT IN A-BOMB DISTANCES, NOT SO FAR YOU'D NOTICE.

BOOZIN' BUDDIES

A fighter pilot lay dying
The medics had left him for dead
All around him women were crying
And these are the words that he said:

"Take the tailpipe out of my stomach
Take the burner out of my brain
Take the turbine out of my kidney
And assemble the unit again.

For we are the boys who fly high in the sky
Bosom buddies while boozin'
We are the boys they send out to die
Bosom buddies while boozin'.

Up in headquarters they sing and they shout
Talking of things they know nothing about!

We are the boys who fly high in the sky
Bosom buddies while boozin'
Bosom buddies while boozin'
Bosom buddies while boozin'."

All air services used the venerable "T-Bird." The first TP-80C (redesignated the T-33A) came off the line in 1947. The ol' "T-Bird" has been with us ever since and many a pilot cut his jet teeth in this fine machine.

REMEMBER...

...A TAKEOFF ATTEMPT WITH THE NOSEWHEEL COCKED?

...SNOW IN THE COCKPIT— *IN JULY?* (IT WAS THE AIR CONDITIONER-PARTICULARLY ON HOT, HUMID DAYS)

...DUCT RUMBLE and OTHER "SPOOK" NOISES?

"VERTICAL FLIGHT AXIS INDICATOR"? (YAW STRING WITH A KNOT IN IT!)

...YOUR VIEW FROM THE REAR SEAT ON FINAL WITH A STUDENT PILOT UP FRONT?

...YOUR FIRST EXPOSURE TO AILERON BOOST?

OUR BOMBER FLIES 10,000 MILES

(Tune: A Gay Caballero)

Our bomber flies ten thousand miles
Our bomber flies ten thousand miles
But a bomb like a cherry
Is all it can carry
When our bomber flies ten thousand miles.

Steady boys, steady boys
Here comes another big lie.
Said pilot to bomber, "How slick
Finding this target's no trick
But my God how strange
We're fresh out of range
Strap on my parachute quick!"

With our bombers the world will be shocked
At three hundred miles they've been clocked
But while dreaming up tricks
With the B-36
We've all had our heads up and locked.

B - 32 DOMINATOR

HEAVY BOMBER

Rivalry between bomber and fighter pilots is legend. A particularly spirited rivalry existed between the 78th Ftr. Gp., based at Duxford, Station 357, and the 91st Bomb Gp. (H), based at Bassingbourn, Station 121, in Jolly Old . . .

IT ALL STARTED WHEN "REDLINE", CANINE MASCOT OF THE 91ST, WAS SPIRITED AWAY DURING A JOINT PARTY.

ROWRF!

SHHH! THROW 'IM ANOTHER BONE!

THE WAR ENDED (WITH "REDLINE" STILL MIA) and THE AIR FORCE GOT BACK TO SPIT and POLISH PARADES—

OH, OH, HERE COMES A 91ST '17 WITH THE BOMB DOORS OPEN.

I DON'T LIKE THE LOOKS OF THIS.

78 FTR GROUP

HORSE MANURE! A HALF TON OF IT!!

THOSE LOUSY ©*!~*!!©*! ...JUST WAIT'LL WE GET THEM!

THE 91ST WAITED WITH BATED BREATH TO SEE WHAT FORM RETALIATION WOULD TAKE. THE NEXT DAY A LONE '51 DROPPED A WREATH AT BASSINGBOURN.

IN MEMORY OF YOUR COMMANDING OFFICER WHO YESTERDAY, OVER DUX-FORD, FELL FROM ONE OF YOUR AIRCRAFT.

IN MEMORIAM

We quote some gems from that venerable Confederate Air Force flight order (issued from "The Octagon" to rebel flight crews for a flight to Wright-Pat. in May 1967.)

PV-I VENTURA

MEDIUM BOMBER
SPAN 65' 6"   LENGTH 51' 9"

THE PREFLIGHT

① Approach the aircraft in a reckless, devil-may-care manner, as this makes a big impression on bystanders. . . . Ask the nearest small boy what type aircraft this is—just to make sure.

② Check all fuel tanks to see if the air has been removed therefrom. Be sure to kick all tires vigorously. When you come to a complicated part of the airplane, stare at it seriously for several seconds. . . . This creates a favorable impression on your crew chief. . . .

③ When you have finished the preflight, ask another bystander what aircraft this is. Then proceed rapidly to your assigned aircraft and repeat steps 1 and 2.

④ To enter the aircraft, approach it from the left side and leap lightly onto the access ladder without looking. Then pick yourself up off the ground in a casual manner, locate the ladder, and climb the steps. . . .

P.S. To control acrophobia, <u>don't look down</u> when going up the ladder!

At the risk of starting a rhubarb with navigators, this story *had* to be told. Equal space is granted on the following pages to navigators who demanded (very vocally, I might add) rebuttal time.

A.D. 1954–

THE WINGS? GLAD YOU ASKED! THEY'RE *MASTER* NAVIGATOR. BRAND NEW CLASSIFICATION—AND ABOUT TIME, TOO! WE NAVIGATORS...

(LONG-TIME FIGHTER JOCK)

BASE OP

...HAVEN'T RECEIVED THE RECOGNITION DUE US! WHY, WITHOUT NAVIGATORS MOST OF THE USAF WOULD BE LOST! THE MAJORITY OF PILOTS I KNOW CAN'T FIND THEIR WAY TO THE LATRINE!

AIRPLANE DRIVERS STILL THINK THE WORLD IS FLAT! WE NAVIGATORS HAVE TO LEAD 'EM BY THE HAND EVERY TIME THEY GET OUTTA SIGHT OF LAND! *furthermore...* BLAH, BLAH, BLAH

BASE OPERATIONS

U.S. AIR FORCE

LISSEN, BIG MOUTH, I GOT 3500 HOURS IN AN AIRPLANE WITHOUT A NAVIGATOR—HOW MANY HAVE YOU GOT WITHOUT A *PILOT*?!

Navigators, zapped on the previous page, responded with vigor. The hail of flak from the Sextant and Bubble Corps about the pint-sized fighter jock is depicted on the facing page.

The years have brought us lows and highs
And long endurance in the skies;
Solid missiles, the sonic boom . . .
And the record sheet has lots more room.

On the following pages we turn from things
With guns and jets and sweptback wings
To some rare old birds, for these "Almanacks" and Airmen's
Dictionaries.

SB2C HELLDIVER

DIVE BOMBER
SPAN 49' 9"   LENGTH 36' 9"

BUZZ JOB
(verb) To fly low. "Cut the grass." Final maneuver practiced by many pilots no longer with us.

FLAT HAT (verb)
To stunt, show off, 'grandstand.' Derived from the old AAF custom of leveling the headgear of 'groundpounder' reviewing stand officers (archaic)

GADGET (noun)
Aviation cadet. Usually found in a position of aggravated brace. According to upperclassmen, something lower than a snake's belly.

TWANNNG!

ULP!

S.O.S. (acronym)
Polite form - 'slop on a shingle'; describes that mixture of creamed (hah!) chipped beef on toast. Usually served on a morning when you had a queasy stomach anyway.

SCARF UP (skarf up) v., From Vietnam. To grab, rescue, capture, as "scarfed up by the Jolly Green Giants." Unfortunately, can also be used as "scarfed up by the V.C."

CLOOGE (.kloogh), n. (Espec. among missile men) Any improvised or makeshift repair, using old tin cans, chewing gum, etc., to simulate first class work in Tech Order compliance. Usual results will not pass close 'eyeball'.

PRANG (prang), v. To damage an aircraft by contact with an immovable object— such as the ground. n. A loud noise accompanying the termination of an aircraft flight; usually preceded by a rapid descent.

'50 MISSION HAT'

RAUNCHY (ronchee), n. Descriptive term usually applied to 2nd Lts., Airmen Basic, and Doolies at the USAF Academy. Contemporary use applies to some college students, most rock-and-roll outfits and all Hippies.

POOR ROBERT'S 'ALMANACK'

1912 - A BUMPER CROP OF NEW AIRCRAFT COMPANIES SPRING UP. AMONG THE MORE NOTABLE WERE: 'CRUMLEY MULTPLANE CO.', 'PEEKSKILL HYDROSEROPLANE CO.', 'REIFLIN HEADLESS AEROPLANE CO.' (IT'S A FACT!)

THIS WAS THE 'BULLET' BUILT BY THE GALLAUDET ENGINEERING CO., SAID TO BE CAPABLE OF FLYING *100 mph!* (WITH A TAILWIND)

JUNE 2, 1924 - U.S. ARMY 'WORLD CRUISERS' BUILT BY DOUGLAS REACH JAPAN (THEY MADE IT CLEAR AROUND THE GLOBE, TOO - *IN 175 DAYS!*)

AUG 17, 1927 - MARTIN JENSEN AND CAPT. PAUL SCHLUTER FLYING THE WRIGHT-POWERED 'ALOHA' ARE SECOND - *AND LAST* - IN THE DOLE OAKLAND-TO-HONOLULU RACE!

(OF 8 ENTRANTS, 4 CRASHED ON TAKEOFF AND 2 WERE LOST AT SEA... HOW ABOUT *THAT* FOR ODDS?!)

1929 FORD MOTOR CO., AIRPLANE DIV., EDSEL FORD PRESIDENT, BUILDS 5-AT MODEL TRI-MOTOR - LATEST IN A LONG SERIES THAT STARTED WITH THE LIBERTY-POWERED STOUT 2-AT

POOR ROBERT'S ALMANACK

DEC 12, 1915

ALL-STEEL "BATTLE PLANE" IS TESTED.

FEB 27, 1920

MAJ. RUDOLPH W. SCHROEDER, IN AN ARMY AIR SERVICE SUPERCHARGED 'LE PERE' AIRCRAFT, SETS AN ALTITUDE RECORD OF 33,113 FT!

JULY 13, 1929

START OF AIRCRAFT ENDURANCE FLIGHT OF FORREST O'BRIEN AND DALE JACKSON IN A CURTIS-ROBIN WHICH BREAKS 400-HR MARK.

JUNE 10, 1948

U.S. AIR FORCE ANNOUNCES THAT CHUCK YEAGER EXCEEDED SPEED OF SOUND IN THE X-1 THE PREVIOUS OCTOBER.

THE AIRMAN'S TOAST

Here's to me in my sober mood
When I ramble, sit and think.
Here's to me in my drunken mood
When I gamble, sin and drink.
And when from this world I pass
I hope they bury me upside down—
So the world can kiss my ass.

INDEX OF SONGS